# Some Black Women

## Profiles of Black Women in Canada

RELLA BRAITHWAITE

TESSA BENN-IRELAND

ISBN 0-920813-84-4

1993 Copyright © Braithwaite, Rella and Tessa Benn-Ireland

All rights reserved. No part of this book may be reproduced or transmitted, in any form or by any means without permission in writing from the publisher, except in the case of reviews.

**Canadian Cataloguing and Publication Data**
Braithwaite, Rella
ISBN 0-920813-84-4
I. Title
FC106.B6B73 1993    305.48'896071    C93-093564-0
F1035.N3B73 1993

Sculpture by: Edna St. Rose
Photographed by: Stephanie Martin
Editor: Jennifer Carter
Editor for Press: Makeda Silvera
Design by Blackbird Design Collective

Grateful acknowledgement is made to the following for Permission to reprint copyrighted material: The Ontario Black History Society, from The Freedom Seekers, by Dr. Dan Hill, (Stoddart Publishing Co. Limited), Multiculturalism program, Government of Canada, Toronto Women's Bookstore (Women of Colour bibliography), and the National Film Board.

Published with the assistance of the Canada Council and the Ontario Arts Council, Minister of Multiculturalism and Citizenship Department of Secretary of State.
The authors wish to thank The Ontario Arts Council for financial assistance.

*Published by*
SISTER VISION
Black Women and Women of Colour Press
P.O. Box 217

DEDICATION

June and Daniel Braithwaite have been an inspiration to me. This book is dedicated to them, in appreciation of their many years of work in the community.

## ACKNOWLEDGEMENTS

We thank you for allowing us to use your profiles, making it possible to update and expand on The Black Woman in Canada and to complete this project Some Black Women: Profiles of Canadian Black Women.

Today we have more role models than ever before and we have tried to feature a cross-section of Black women, some actively working, as well as those who have contributed significantly in the pass.

We would especially like to express our gratitude to Verda Cook, Lyly Kersey and Aileen Benn for their continuous support.

Thanks to our editor Jennifer Carter and all the other women involved in the production of this book. Finally we would like to extend our gratitude to Makeda Silvera, who believed in the project when the materials were still scraps of paper, for her vision, and for her commitment and work to see that process through from 1989 to the publication of this book in 1993.

EDITOR'S NOTE

This book was written as an introduction to some of the outstanding Black women in Canada. By no means is it an inclusive list of significant Black women. The information was compiled by the authors through a series of interviews with the women portrayed. It is not intended to be used as an authoritative piece of scolasticism. It is hoped that the book will give the reader the incentive to learn more about the Black community.

PUBLISHER'S NOTE

The publishers of this commemorative book of Black Women in Canada regret that some of the photographs are not of the highest quality. However, they are historical mementos and therefore important to preserve.

# TABLE OF CONTENTS

Introduction     **8**

Profiles of Black Women     **9**

Women and Black Churches     **46**

Women's Organizations     **54**

The Early Black Church     **60**

The Black Media     **64**

Early Black Organizations     **72**

Black Landmarks Site     **74**

Bursaries Awards in Names of Outstanding Blacks     **82**

Film and Video by Black Women     **90**

Some Books by Sister Vision: Black Women and Women of Colour     **94**

More Books by Black Canadian Women     **98**

Quick Facts on Blacks     **102**

# INTRODUCTION

Blacks have lived in Canada since the time of slavery. After England abolished the slave trade in Upper Canada in 1793, Black refugees fled to the United States. During World War One, the Canadian government set definite limits on Black immigration to Canada. In 1953, the Canadian government agreed to an annual immigration of one hundred women from Jamaica and Barbados to work in Canadian homes as domestics. By 1960, the number had increased to three hundred. Many women from the islands were anxious to come to Canada to improve their education and skills while working at jobs they would not have accepted in their own countries. Until the 1960s, the majority of Black women made their living as domestic workers.

Black women whose families have been in Canada for several generations, understand how it feels to be excluded from the mainstream of society. We must not forget the men and women who helped pave the way for the newcomers.

Black women, whether native-born or from other countries, have contributed to the professions, the arts and the community at large. Despite the differences in our birthplaces, we experience the double oppression of being Black and woman. This fact makes it all the more important for us as Black women to document our lives, experiences and contributions to Black history. Working within existing organizations and forming new ones will give us a united voice in Canadian society. While we face many challenges such as poverty, depression and isolation, we must remain strong, vibrant and confident.

# PROFILES OF BLACK WOMEN

## A SALUTE TO BLACK WOMEN ACHIEVERS

In the following pages, you will be introduced to some very special women. Politicians, educators, religious leaders, artists, businesswomen, and social activists. Considering their diverse careers, one might assume that these individuals would have little in common. Upon closer analysis of these women, it becomes apparent that there is a great deal to share.

These women are African-Canadians. They may have been born in the Caribbean, Africa, America or Canada, but each of their ancestors came from Africa. Consequently, they all belonged to the same community.

These outstanding individuals were all proud of their heritage. Some of them were discouraged from going to school and many of them encountered overt racism. These women took their negative experiences and made them positive.

As a result of their struggle these Black women, learnt a very valuable lesson. They learned how to SURVIVE! They realized that in order to succeed, they would have to be twice as good as the next person.

Each of these individuals recognized the importance of an education. Whether they were self-educated or institutionally schooled, they understood that knowledge was the key to advancement.

They accepted life as a great gift, not because of what it gave them, but because of what it enabled them to give to others. No matter how successful these women became, they remained dedicated to their families, the church and the community. More than anything else, these women were true to themselves!

Hopefully, after reading this book, you will have learned a little bit more about some of the outstanding women in the community. Perhaps some of them wll be particularly interesting to you. Go out and learn more about them. Get involved in the organizations in the community. Only by learning more about your history, will you be able to move forward. Be proud of your heritage as an African Canadian and don't ever let anyone tell you that you aren't good enough! You can do anything if you set your mind to it!

Live your dreams!!!

## JEAN AUGUSTINE

In 1988, Jean Augustine was appointed Chairman of Metro Toronto Housing Authority. She was born in St. George's the capitol of Grenada. When she arrived in Canada in 1959, Augustine was a qualified teacher but under the immigration rules of the day, she was required to work a year as a domestic. She put herself through school in Toronto, working as a babysitter and a shoe clerk. She received her Ontario Teacher's certificate, graduated from University of Toronto and earned a Master of Education degree from the Ontario Institute for Studies in Education. She became principal of Etobicoke's St. Gregory Separate School.

Jean is dedicated to improving the conditions of over 125,000 tenants. On taking over the agency with a budget of $200 million, Augustine vowed to improve situations in Metro Housing and immediately launched an anti-drug campaign for the agency's 110 housing projects.

## AUDREY BARNES

The church has been instrumental in cultivating social services. Audrey Barnes was a member of the British Methodist Episcopal Church (BME) since 1954 and has served as the President of the local Missionary Society. As the President of the Conference Missionary Society, Barnes has served on foreign and home missions.

Through her unselfish work, she has helped many needy individuals and become an inspiration for all.

## CARRIE BEST

During the late 1940s, Carrie Best co-founded a newspaper entitled The Clarion which later became a national paper called the Negro Citizen. Best was born in New Glasgow, Nova Scotia in 1903. Her great-grandparents came to Nova Scotia from the United States in 1787. A former teacher, journalist and broadcaster, Best was actively involved in the struggle for human and civil rights. In recognition of her many contributions to society, she was awarded the Order of Canada in 1975. Best was also selected as an Officer of the Order and received an Honourary Doctorate of Law from Saint Francis Xavier University in Nova Scotia. Best was also presented the Lloyd McInnis Memorial Award, the National Black Award and the Harry Jerome Award for community service. In 1988, the `Carrie Best Mobile Library,' a collection of books by Black writers, was established in her name in Ottawa.

## ROSEMARY BROWN

In 1972, Rosemary Brown became the first Black woman in Canada to win a seat in a Legislative Assembly. A Jamaican-born Canadian, Brown has a Bachelor of Arts degree from McGill University and a Master of Social Work from the University of British Columbia. Commended for her work in social politics and feminism, Brown holds an Honourary Doctorate in Humane Letters from Mount St. Vincent University. In recognition of her outstanding work in the legal field, Brown has been granted Honourary Doctorates in Law from York University, Dalhousie and the University of Toronto. This exemplary woman was awarded a Human Rights Fellowship from the United Nations, the Queen's Commemorative Medal and the 1987 Woman of Distinction Award from the YWCA. Brown's autobiography entitled Being Brown: A Very Public Life was published in 1989 by Ballentine Books. In 1992, a biography for young people called Brown Girl in the Ring was published by Sister Vision, Black Women and Women of Colour Press.

## ZANANA AKANDE

Zanana Akande was the first Black woman to hold a cabinet post in the Ontario Government. She grew up in Toronto and has had a distinguished career as an educator, as well as being involved in community organizations including the United Way of Greater Toronto and the Ontario Teachers' Federation. Before entering politics, Akande served as the Principal of George Syme Public School in Toronto. She was elected to provincial Parliament for the New Democrat Party on September 6, 1990. Akande is currently the Parliamentary Assistant to Premier Bob Rae.

## SALOME BEY

Born in Newark, New Jersey, the dynamic Salome Bey came to Canada in 1964 and has made unique contributions as an actress, singer, playwright and composer. As well as her many albums, her long list of credits include a television special and performances in Canada, the United States and Europe. On broadway, Bey has appeared in musicals such as `Don't Bother Me, I Can't Cope,' `Duds' and `Your Arm's Too Short To Box With God.'

Bey has written several musical cabarets including the Dora Mavis Moore winner, `Indigo', `Madame Gertrude,' `Shimmytime' and `Sweet Mama', based on the life of Ethel Waters. She has worked throughout the United States, directing a host of productions such as `For Coloured Girls,' and `The Diary of Anne Frank.'

Her New York production of `Love Me, Love My Children,' brought her an Obie Award and she has been the three-time Canadian winner of the *Cheer* Black Music Award.

Bey frequently performs at benefits, such as the Amnesty International concert in Toronto in 1989, which  generated funds for the release of political prisoners who were incarcerated for their writings.

## ANNE COOLS

As a child, growing up in Barbados, Anne Cools learned two very valuable lessons from her parents. First, society owes no one anything. Secondly, we all have a responsibility to contribute to society. Cools attended Queen's College in Barbados and McGill University in Montreal. She later worked as the Executive Director of Women In Transition, a shelter for battered women and their children in Toronto. Through hard work and dedication, Anne Cools became the first Black person to be appointed to the Senate of Canada on January 13, 1984.

## VIOLET BLACKMAN

Violet Blackman was one of the founding members of the United Negro Improvement Association (UNIA) which was initiated by Marcus Garvey in 1916. The UNIA was dedicated to the advancement of Blacks around the world and in the 1920s, it was the largest Black organization. For many years, Blackman shared her home with new arrivals from the Caribbean and helped them study and obtain work. She spent most of her life in organizations and her only ambition was to help those in need.

The Jamaican native received numerous tributes for her outstanding contribution to society. In 1989, she was presented the Order of Ontario in recognition of her service to the Black community. She also received the Jerome Award and the Ontario Award of Merit which was presented by Premier Frank Miller. In 1972, the UNIA presented Blackman with a self-portrait in honour of her fifty years membership, her service as President

and her contribution to the Garvey Movement. Mrs. Blackman passed away in 1990.

## THELMA POWELL-BROWN

Thelma Powell-Brown founded the Powell-Brown Therapeutic Nursery School in Toronto in 1965. This organization was designed to provide treatment for hyperactive and mildly retarded children. After receiving a grant from the government, Brown moved the school from the basement of the Faith Lutheran Church to a much larger building in Downsview. The Children's Centre soon became one of the most respected centres for pre-school children in Toronto. By 1980, Powell-Brown was operating a range of services out of Sheppard Public School, providing referrals, services for children, infant stimulation programs, as well as advice for ethnic and multi-cultural concerns for the Metropolitan Toronto area.

During her distinguished career, Powell-Brown received Ontario's Good Citizenship Award, the City of Toronto's Centennial Medal and North York's Municipal Medal. She was also the recipient of the Queen's Silver Jubilee Medal as well as a plaque from Governor General, Jules Legere.

## PEGGY DOWNES

Major Peggy Downes was born in Dartmouth, Nova Scotia. She joined the Royal Canadian Army Service Corps Militia in 1955. For fifteen years, Downes was the only female member of the Negro Colour Guard attaining the rank of Master Warrant Officer. Her outstanding work in the military was recognized in 1968 when she was awarded the Canadian Forces Decoration. In 1980, Downes became the first female Honourary Aide de Camp to Ontario Lieutenant Governor John Black Aird. In recognition of her dedication to the Canadian Forces, Downes was appointed Officer of the Order of Military Merit in 1988.

## ALICE DARRELL

Alice Darrell came to Toronto in 1947 with her husband Alec Darrell and their four children. She then enroled in Toronto Bible College, in a four-year night course, ending in 1951. By then she was a mother of seven children.

"Since the needle and thread was a must in my life, I registered at Central Technical School in tailoring. I sewed for my family, as well as for financial reasons. Later I enroled at Northern Technical School in ceramics, cake decorating, gift wrapping.

Darrell joined the Eureka Friendly Club in 1950 and served as president for over twenty-five years. Darrell was the first married women to be elected in her church, and served for fifteen years.

I still found time for community involvement in the United Appeal, Red Cross, Heart Fund, Cancer Society, Salvation Army, Cubs, Brownies, as well as visiting what was then known as "999 Queen Street Hospital" with a friend.

"By 1955 my youngest was attending school. I felt the need to ease away from home sewing and launch out in a wider field.

"After taking an extensive course in bone structure, anatomy, the posture of the body-specifically the fitting, measuring and description of foundations described by doctors to be made for their clients. I was able to fit the obese as well as the disabled men and women with foundation garments, it became a great joy for me to see people happy because of my service".

## VIVAN CHAVIS

Vivian Chavis was the author of the book entitled Musical Buxton which was published in conjunction with the 1969 Labour Day celebration in Buxton. Chavis documented the history of the early musical groups and individuals who spiritually enhanced the lives of Buxtonites. She believed that music was a great unifying force for the Black community. An early member of the Ontario History Society, Vivian Chavis was a regional executive member when she passed away in 1983.

## VERA CUDJOE

For Vera Cudjoe, the desire to educate in an entertaining fashion, has been an endless endeavour. Before 1973, Vera Cudjoe had a dream. She wanted a theatre for Blacks. To tell their stories and teach their history. She wanted an organization that would represent the Black community in an effort to share and enjoy. Cudjoe founded Black Theatre Canada and worked as the artistic director. Cudjoe used theatre as a means of informing, entertaining and uniting the Black community. The company staged many successful performances, workshops and seminars. In 1988, the Trinidadian-born Cudjoe co-wrote 'The Story of Mary Ann Shadd,' a biography of one of Canada's most significant Black pioneers. In 1978, she received the Queen's Canadian Silver Jubilee Award as well as the Caribbean Cultural Achievement Award. The Association of Black Women also recognized Cudjoe's achievements when they presented her with the Outstanding Award. Regretfully, Black Theatre Canada suspended operations and closed its doors in 1988 because of lack of funding.

## JEAN DANIELS

Daniels grew up in Nova Scotia. A dressmaker by profession, she worked in a hat factory during World War II, but always remained active in Black community projects. She later moved to Toronto and joined a group called the 'Open Door Club.' The newspaper, Canadian Negro, grew out of this group. It was published between 1953 to 1958 and was distributed across Canada from Vancouver to Halifax. Jean Daniels was the President of the Anti-Apartheid Committee for ten years. This organization provided financial assistance for Blacks in South Africa. Funds were raised through dinners and lectures with guest speakers coming from the United States and South Africa in order to provide encouragement and assistance for the humanitarian venture. Daniels was also actively involved in the founding of the Library of Black Literature and served on its Board of Directors. In 1973, Daniels received the National Black Award for her outstanding contribution to the community. Jean Daniels passed away in 1978.

## BEV FOLKES

Bev Folkes a Jamaican born parent of three, has worked for fifteen years with the community in various capacities: counsellor, race and ethnic relations worker, conductor of training and development seminars, administrator, and resource person.

As well as being actively involved in community work, Bev also feels strongly about the educational system and where Black students fit in - "I don't think people are looking at the serious flaws of our education. They are not aware of the streamlining process that's happening to our West Indian kids...there is a vast amount of them in vocational schools". As a result of this concern, Bev bid, in 1978, for the Ward 3 School Trustee position but was unsuccessful.

In 1981, Bev became involved in working with the Black Inmates and Friends Assembly - where she started out counselling inmates who were soon to be released, as well as arranging programmes, and visitation. Bev has continued her work within the correctional system and serves as a Liaison Coordinator for Inmates in five Federal Institution.

## MAVIS ELAINE BURKE

Mavis Elaine Burke has had an extensive academic career. Born in Jamaica, she attended the University of the West Indies where she majored in history. She obtained a Masters in Education from the University of London then completed a Ph.D. in Education from the University of Ottawa. Her doctoral dissertation `An Analysis of Canadian Aid to Education in the Commonwealth Caribbean Leeward and Windward Islands,' forms part of a lengthy list of published works on education and curriculum development.

Burke became a special consultant in immigrant education, designing a curriculum for foreign students and educators with the Toronto Board of Education. From 1977-1981, Burke worked as the Education Officer with the Ministry of Education at Queen's Park. She chaired several committees which studied the racial, religious and cultural bias apparent in school materials.

She became the President of the Ontario Advisory Council on Multiculturalism in 1984. Burke also chaired the Ontario Assistance Review Board which was made up of thirty-one government appointed members. In 1987, she served as the special advisor of Minority Women's Issues at the Ontario Women's Directorate.

This highly respected woman continues to be involved in the Black community in organizations such as the Ontario Black Historical Society, the School-A-Child Program and the Jamaican Canadian Association.

In recognition of her achievements, Burke has received many awards. She has been granted a fellowship from the Ontario Institute for Studies in Education. Burke was also presented the National Award for achievement in Multiculturalism and the Award of Excellence for professional service in Canada from Air Jamaica.

## ALICE VERNA CHATTERS

Alice Verna Chatters was a fifth generation Canadian, born in Dresden, Ontario at the turn of the century to George and Effie Kersey. She was the first Black woman to be elected President of the Windsor Local Council of Women and was honoured with both local and national life memberships. In 1950, she chaired the Housing and Town Planning and Citizenship Committee at the United Nations Symposium on Human Rights. Chatters was the President of the Hour A Day Club and a Director of the YWCA.

## RITA COX

Seldom is a librarian held in such high regard as Rita Cox. The avid reader was born in Trinidad where she met Augusta Baker, the internationally renowned storyteller. Baker arranged for Cox to study Children's Librarianship in New York at Columbia University. She became the Head Librarian of the Parkdale Library. She has launched multi-cultural and international festivals during her seventeen years at the library. She has coordinated educational lectures, films and art exhibits in order to offer insight into the lifestyles and cultures of other lands. Cox established a program called 'Project Read' which was designed to encourage literacy and academic excellence in the Parkdale community. Specially trained volunteers were sent into the neighbourhood offering reading and writing tutorials. She has served on the Ontario Council of Multiculturalism and Citizenship. In 1984, Cox coordinated the highly successful festival of Black Heritage and Storytelling. She has appeared on television and has told her stories throughout Canada, England and the Caribbean.

Cox has been awarded the Ontario Bicentennial Medal for her service to the community. In 1982, she was presented Canada's Birthday Achievement Award

## DR. INEZ ELLISTON

Dr. Elliston was the first Co-ordinator of the Multiculturalism and Race Relations Committee of the Scarborough Board of Education. She was responsible for the implementation of fourteen major policy recommendations, including multicultural training for staff and improved assessment of immigrant children in the school system. She has been dedicated to integration of students from diverse backgrounds and hopes that one day, all children will receive the same educational opportunity. In April, 1989, Elliston was called to Ottawa where she was presented the federal Citizenship Award.

## KAMALA JEAN GOPIE

For Kamala Gopie, activity has been the key to life. When she was not busy teaching elementary school, she was earnestly involved in any number of pursuits. Born in Jamaica, Gopie arrived in Canada in 1963. In an effort to keep ties alive, she quickly became involved with the Jamaican Canadian Association. It was the first of many local, provincial, national and international organizations with which she was to become acquainted over the next twenty-six years. Gopie has worked as a consultant on equity in the curriculum with the North York Board of Education and has served on race relations task forces. She was the President of the International Social Service of Canada and served as the Chairperson of the Equal Opportunity Committee of the Toronto Mayor's Committee on Race Relations for four years.

## LORRAINE HUBBARD

For several years Lorraine Hubbard has made an invaluable contribution to the Black and wider community by setting up Black History workshops, exhibits, and providing instruction on taping procedures. As an executive member of the Ontario Black History Society she spend a great deal of time researching, writing and putting on exhibits for schools libraries, and the general public.

While Executive-Director of the OBHS Hubbard produced and directed a 20 minute video on the 200 year history of Blacks in Ontario. The video, A Proud Past - A Promising Future, examines several periods of history beginning with the introduction of slavery to Upper Canada, and the contributions of Blacks in modern Canada.

A founding member of the society, and also a great grand-daughter of William Hubbard, she resigned in 1985, but continued to assist the OBHS.

## DAURENE LEWIS

In 1984, Daurene Lewis became the first Black woman in Canada to be elected mayor. Lewis is a descendent of James Fortune, a freed slave who accompanied British Empire Loyalists fleeing the United States in 1783. In her early years, she had considered becoming a doctor, but Nova Scotia's early history of racial discrimination led her to train as a nurse. Several years before running for mayor, she gave up nursing and opened a craft and clothing shop in Annapolis Royal. Lewis became the mayor of the predominantly white town of Annapolis Royal, winning eighty percent of the vote.

## TILLY MAYS

Tilly Mays was one of the spirited women who formed the Benevolent Club, later named the Coloured Women's Club. She was one of nine children born to George and Frances Tousaint-Jones of Montreal in the 1870s. Her father and brother ran the first black barbershop in Montreal on McGill Street. Mays worked tirelessly with the soldiers who had returned from the Boer War. She provided soup kitchens, rolled bandages for the wounded and provided temporary homes. An original member of the Union United Church, 'Aunt Tilly' also worked with Sunday school children for over forty-five years.

## ARLIE ROBBINS

Arlie C. Robbins was the curator of the Raleigh Township Centennial Museum and spent many years researching the history of the Elgin Settlement. In her book entitled Legacy to Buxton, this outstanding writer traced the history of many of the families which were involved in the Buxton community and other Black settlements in Ontario. She completed the history of the Grand Lodge of Ontario and Jurisdiction. Robbins was the Past Grand Conductor of the Order of the Eastern Star of Ontario. She was awarded the Centennial Medal in recognition of her contribution to the Black history of Kent County. An accomplished artist, Robbin's works are widely displayed. Her painting entitled 'The Last Supper,' hangs in front of the BME Church. Arlie Robbins passed away in 1985.

## ROSE FORTUNE

Long before the feminist movement in Canada, a Black woman Rose Fortune, calmly invaded the male world and was policewoman and "baggage smasher" in Annapolis Royal, a seaport town in the Annapolis Valley of Nova Scotia.

She elected herself policewoman on the continent and none denied her the right, as she ruled a strong, powerful arm of the law and operated a transfer company which established a precedent.

She was born in 1774 and her parents came to Annapolis Valley as slaves of the Devonne family. Rose was to be on deck with her transfer wagon which was really a stout wheelbarrow. As a baggage-smasher, Fortune trudged to and fro pushing the heavy leads of trunks parcels between the hotel and the wharf.

It is believed she started her business about 1825 until it became an established company called the Lewis Transfer in 1841, when horse-drawn wagons were used. This business was later carried on by Rose Fortune's direct descendants for one hundred and twenty-five years.

A daughter, which was one of two born to Rose Fortune married John Francis of Digby and their daughter married Albert Lewis. Offspring from this union, James and Oscar Lewis founded the Lewis Transfer (1841). The company operated in the Lewis family until 1965 when it was sold to a White Nova Scotian but the name remained the same.

## MICHELINE A. RAWLINS

Judge Micheline Rawlins was admitted to the Bar in London, Ontario in 1982. She became an Ontario Court judge in Windsor, Ontario's Provincial Division in 1992. Her Honour Judge Rawlins is the first Black Woman to be appointed to an Ontario court bench.

A Mother of two children, Rawlins was born in Montreal where she received a B.A. at McGill University, in Political Science and Sociology. She studied Law at the University of Windsor and served as Assisted Crown Attorney in Kent County, Chathman from 1986 to 1992. Judge Rawlins has served on numerous boards and committees.

## JENNIFER HODGE DE SILVA

Jennifer Hodge de Silva became a film producer because she believed that ordinary people needed a vehicle for expressing themselves. She was the associate producer of Fields of Endless Day, a documentary of the struggles and triumphs of Canada's Black population. Co-produced by the National Film Board and the Ontario Education Communications Authority, this film covered 300 years of Black Canadian history. In 1983, Hodge directed Home Feeling: Struggle for a Community. This controversial film portrayed the Blacks in the Jane and Finch area of Toronto. The Fine Arts graduate from York University became a CBC producer in 1982. Marrying Paul De Silva, the couple created a series entitled Inside Stories which portrayed the lives of Torontonians from various ethnic backgrounds.

In May 1989, the talented young film maker passed away after battling a lengthy illness. Hodge was the daughter of Mairuth Hodge-Sarsfield and the granddaughter of Mr. and Mrs. Packwood.

## HAZEL SHARP PITTMAN

Hazel Pittman was born in Toronto, in 1888, eldest daughter of the late Charles and Serena Sharp. She attended Palmerston Ave., Louisa and Borden St. Schools, and was brought up in the British Methodist Episcopal Church in Toronto.

She married Thomas Pittman in 1936. Hazel became active in the church at the age of thirteen, taught class, belonged to Auxiliaries, sang in the Choir, and was ordained as a Deaconess in 1959 by the late Rev. I.H. Edwards and the late Dr. A.S. Markham. Mrs. Pittman, an early member of the Eureka Club, passed away in March 1976.

## MAIRUTH HODGE-SARSFIELD

The distinguished career of Mairuth Hodge-Sarsfield encompassed many areas including broadcasting, diplomacy, advertising and marketing. The Montreal native served on the Board of Directors of the Canadian Broadcasting Corporation since 1984. This outstanding woman also worked as a senior information officer for the United Nations' Environment Program in Nairobi and New York. She produced the widely acclaimed U.N.E.P. program, "For Every Child a Tree." The city of Cleveland proclaimed October 22, 1982 Mairuth Sarsfield Day in recognition of outstanding achievements of this exemplary woman.

## DR. GLENDA SIMMS

In 1989, Glenda Simms was appointed President of the Canadian Advisory Council on the Status of Women. Born in Jamaica, Simms has been dedicated to the advancement of minority women. She believes feminism is about independence, self-reliance, choices and knowledge about self-esteem and speaking out for change. She was the President of the Congress of Black Women and is currently on leave from the Faculty of Education at Nipissing University. The Federal Government presented Simms with a Citation for Citizenship in recognition of her dedication to women's issues.

## BEVERLY MASCOLL

Beverly Mascoll is the President of Mascoll Beauty Supply Ltd., a company that specializes in beauty products for the black consumer. Since Mascoll couldn't find suitable makeup for herself, she decided to open her own cosmetics business which would cater to women of colour. Originally, this was a small company which Mascoll ran from her home. The company has been quite successful and Mascoll has opened an International Beauty Complex on Bathurst St. in Toronto. In 1985, the Association of Black Women presented Mascoll the Award of Achievement for her `admirable contribution to the black community'.

## SHERENE SHAW

Guyanese-born Sherene Shaw worked as a volunteer in many community organizations before entering the political arena. Throughout her work as a counsellor for troubled youth, fundraiser for disabled children and UNICEF volunteer coordinator, Shaw realized that it was necessary to become involved in the decision-making process in order to bring about changes. In 1988, she was elected to the Scarborough Council.

## DOROTHY ABIKE WILLS

This outstanding scholar and educator was born on the island of Dominica. She came to Canada to attend Mount Saint Vincent University. In 1956, she received a Bachelor of Science Degree and went on to complete a Masters in Social Work and a Ph.D. from Pacific Western University in California.

She has taught at Vanier College and Concordia University while also working as a Social Worker in several Montreal institutions. In 1984, Wills developed the curriculum for the Special Care Counselling program at Vanier College. This program was implemented at the Kahnawake Reserve and enabled the people of the First Nation to work with their own populations.

In 1987, Dorothy developed a mentor program which was aired on CBC Radio. By pairing young people with professionals, role models were created.

She was appointed to the Immigration and Refugee Board of Canada in 1988. Wills has travelled extensively and has studied in both East and West Africa. She represented Canada in Lagos, Nigeria at the planning meetings of the International Festival for the Second World Black and African Festival of Arts and Culture. She has done post-graduate studies in East and West African History and Culture at Howard University, Washington.

Among her many awards, Wills has received the National Black Coalition of Canada Community Award, the Dominica Island Association Outstanding Award, and the Mount Saint Vincent University Alumna Jubilee Award of Distinction Medal. In 1989, Wills was appointed to the Order of Canada for her outstanding contribution to the Canadian Black community. That same year, Wills received an Honourary Doctor of Law Degree from Concordia University.

## MAXINE TYNES

Maxine Tynes is a writer, poet and freelance broadcaster who is a lifelong resident of Dartmount, N.S. Her heritage goes back to the time of the Black Loyalists in Nova Scotia. In 1986 Tynes co-wrote and performed in a documentary drama based on the death of Stephen Biko, a Black freedom fighter in South Africa. She has won numerous awards and is in great demand as a lecturer.

## CHRISTINA JENKINS HOWSON

Christina Jenkins Howson was born in Chatham, Ontario in 1987 to Michael and Elizabeth De Groat. She co-founded the Black paper entitled Dawn of Tomorrow with her husband James F. Jenkins. The paper was first published in London, Ontario in 1923 and was believed to be the most successful of all Black newspapers. Upon her husband's death in 1931, Howson assumed full editorial responsibilities. By 1950, the local newspaper was circulating beyond Canadian borders. The fact that Howson edited a highly successful Black paper was an incredible achievement for a woman at the time. However, her accomplishments went far beyond her career.

Howson was a devoted humanitarian, active in community and church affairs. When asked to consider running for the office of alderperson, she graciously declined saying she did not wish to deprive her family of her care and consideration. Howson had re-married but found herself widowed again in 1955. She was faced with the task of

working as the editor and raising nine children. She accepted the challenge and raised a family who had a love for education and were also active in the community.

In 1967, Howson passed away, but her legacy lives on. The London-based paper has continued to be published periodically by the family members.

## VERDA COOK

Verda Cook was born in Toronto, the great-granddaughter of a slave who came to Canada on the Underground Railway. She was a founding member of both the Congress of Black Women in Toronto and the National Black Coalition. When Cook was growing up, she was discouraged from continuing her schooling and told that she would find employment only in domestic work. Nonetheless, she continued to attend school. She became a member of the Board of Directors of the first Caribana Celebration in 1967 and served as a Regional Director of the Canadian Sickle Cell Association for three years. Cook also served on the Ontario Black History Society's Board of Directors. In 1977, Cook received the Queen's Medal in recognition of her service to the Black community. She was honoured by the Association of Black Women for her achievements in 1983.

## JUANITA WESTMORELAND-TRAORE

Canadian-born Juanita Westmoreland-Traore has been recognized internationally for her efforts to gain greater equality for women, Blacks, and visible minorities. She was appointed Employment Equity Commissioner by the Ontario government in 1991. Her specialization in public law, made Westmoreland-Traore an ideal candidate for this position. After graduating from the University of Montreal Faculty of Law, she completed a Doctorate of State in Public Law at the University of Paris. From 1976-1985, Westmoreland-Traore worked as a professor of administrative, constitutional and municipal law at the University of Montreal. Westmoreland-Traore also worked part-time as the Commissioner of the Canadian Human Rights from 1983-1985. She became the President of the Conseil des Communatues Culturelle et de l'Immigration in 1985. This highly successful career woman was also active in the Black community, serving as the Chairperson of the Montreal Regional Committee of the Congress of Black Women.

## BERNICE LOBEL CARNEGIE REDMON

In 1941, studying nursing was not a possibility for young Black women in Canada. Determined to become a nurse, Redmon enroled in the St. Philip School of Nursing at the Medical College of Virginia. Upon completing the nursing program, she returned to Canada and became the first Black nurse hired by the Toronto Victorian Order of Nurses. Throughout the time she spent in nursing, Redmon continued to upgrade her skills and participate in community groups. She taught Sunday school and sung in several choirs. She was also a member of the Eureka Friendly Club which was one of the oldest chartered clubs in Canada.

## ERMA COLLINS

Erma Collins served as the chairperson of the English and Liberal Arts Department of the St. James Campus of George Brown College in Toronto for many years. She directed the teaching of English and Social Science courses while also supervising thirty-three contract faculty members. In addition, she developed and monitored sixty post-secondary and manpower courses in English, French and the Social Sciences. Collins has also served as the Executive Secretary on the Jamaican-Canadian Association Committee. She has worked as a volunteer teacher with the Black Education Project as well as the Black Heritage Program. Collins founded the Singles' Club for Mature West Indians and acted as president from 1979 to 1982.

## KAY LIVINGSTONE

Kay Livingstone devoted her life to reducing social prejudice. At a Women's International meeting in 1975, Livingstone noticed that she was the only woman of colour present and notified the federal government. She coined the phrase 'visible minority' and used it to refer to individuals of Black, Asian or Indian descent. Shortly after this incident, she was appointed as a one-woman investigative committee of minority womens' issues. Livingstone travelled across the country, contacting organizations for women of colour and informing them of their rights. She was born in London, Ontario. Her Cayuga-born parents, James and Christina Jenkins, founded The Dawn of Toronto.

In 1973, Livingstone coordinated the first National Congress of Black Women in Canada. She was also a successful radio broadcaster with programs on the CBC, CKEY, and CFTR. In 1950, Livingstone founded the Canadian Negro Women's Association. She worked as an advocate of the Black community until her death in 1974.

## CLEATA MORRIS

Cleata Morris was born in Raleigh Township near North Buxton, Ontario. Her teaching career began in September, 1944 at S.S. 10 Chatham Township, a one room rural school with an enrolment of forty-five students from grades one to eight. In 1958, she worked as a primary teacher with the Windsor Board of Education at John Campbell, Bondy and Northwood Schools. She has worked on committees which developed a Primary Social Studies Curriculum Guide, a Reading Guide for the Primary Division and a course in Black Studies for use in grades seven to thirteen.

## ANNE PACKWOOD

Anne Packwood founded the Coloured Women's Club in Montreal. In 1956, she became conscious of the special needs of multiracial children and presented a series of talks on child care which were aired on CBC Radio. She was honoured with a special award from the City of Montreal for her continuous care for foster children from 1926-1966. In 1978, Packwood was featured in the film entitled Fields of Endless Day. At the age of ninety-seven, Packwood received the Wazee Award at the Many Rivers to Cross Exhibition.

Wazee is a Swahili word meaning 'elder.'

## EDNA TUITT

At a time when there was great difficulty placing Black children in foster homes, 'Ma Tuitt' took at least fifty of them into her care. To each child, she gave love, attention and discipline. No distinction was ever made between foster children and her own. They all shared the same duties, food, living space and love. In 1963, Tuitt was named 'Mother of the Year' by the Montreal Canadian Pacific Railway Ladies' Auxiliary. Today, more than forty years later, Tuitt's former foster children still visit her regularly.

## AILEEN WILLIAMS

Aileen WIlliams was the founding Secretary of the Canadian Negro Women's Association. She also served as the Secretary on a four member Steering Committee for the original Congress of Black Women in Canada. She is currently involved in a Steering Committee collating materials for a book outlining the twenty-five year history of the Canadian Negro Women's Association. Williams is a sixth generation Canadian whose paternal grandmother was a descendent of the Eddy family of Oro township settlement in Oro, Ontario.

## MARGUERITE JACKSON WILSON

Marguerite Jackson Wilson, daughter of the late Gen. Superintendent, Rev. Jackson of the British Methodist Episcopal Church has been active in the B.M.E Church all her life. She has had the distinction of serving the Toronto Church for more than twenty years. She was the founding president of the Senior Citizens Club of Christ Church B.M.E. and past president of the Women's Home and Foreign Missionary Society. She also served churches at London and Windsor.

In 1975 Marguerite married Reverend Wilson, pastor of B.M.E. churches in Owen Sound and Collingwood. Marguerite who was born in Dresden, Ontario was honoured along with three dedicated members by the Ladies League in 1984 for serving the church over half a century. Marguerite Jackson Wilson passed away December 1992.

## IRIS WILLIAMS

Rev. Iris Williams of Oakville, Ontario, who has a passion for helping people in the Caribbean, Haiti and North America, is an Evangelist of the African Methodist Episcopal Church. She is founder of Todd's Road A.M.E. Church and Nesta Patrick Nursery School in Trinidad and in Haiti, she founded Citi Solia A.M.E. Mission and another Nesta Patrick Nursery School. This Trinidad-born Minister runs her own ministry and commutes between Trinidad and the United States, Britain, Canada and other Caribbean Islands participating in A.M.E. functions as an Evangelist or operating her nursery schools. Nine years ago Rev. Williams became permanent resident in Canada and applied to her Church superior in Trinidad for transfer papers that would enable her to minister here. She was soon part in Grant A.M.E. Church, Toronto. She also served a two-year term at Oakville's Turner Chapel A.M.E. Rev. Iris Williams has a dedication and willingness to further the kingdom of God by Outreach programs and fundraising drives which she frequently organizes.

## LOUISE ROCK

Louise Rock's name is distinguished for her work in the field of musical education for retarded children. In 1952, Rock became a charter member of the Windsor Association for Retarded Children. Caring for her own child who suffered from multiple sclerosis, gave her special insight into the problems of the disabled and their families. She volunteered to teach music to the class of mentally retarded children in Windsor. She lead seminars, conventions and summer courses for teachers of the trainable retarded. Upon retiring from teaching in 1972, Rock was awarded a Life Membership in the Ontario Association. That same year, the mayor of Windsor recognized her unselfish contribution to the community by selecting her as Citizen of the Week. In 1986, Louise Rock passed away.

## ROSETTA AMOS RICHARDSON

For many years, Rosetta Amos Richardson was one of the oldest members of Toronto's Black community. Rosetta and her husband, Samuel Cromwell Richardson, owned and operated the first Soul Food Restaurant in Toronto in 1891. With the experience gained from the successful venture, Richardson proceeded to establish a Lunch Counter at the Canadian National Exhibition, the first Black person to take on such a task. She was also a devoted member of the BME Church and actively participated in the Missionary Society. From her large family came a grand-daughter, Gwen Johnston, co-owner of the Third World Bookstore. Mrs. Richardson died in 1953 in her ninety-sixth year.

## GWENDOLYN A. JOHNSTON

Gwendolyn Johnston co-founded the Toronto Third World Bookstore twenty years ago with her husband. They promoted the work of Canadian and Third World writers, while also hosting art shows. Johnston has offered artists encouragement, support and honest advice. The bookstore has become a forum for diverse literature as well as artistic exhibits.

## DOROTHY SHADD SHREVE

Dorothy Shadd Shreve was the author of Pathfinders of Liberty and Truth and The African Canadian Church: A Stabilizer, the Positive Role of the Black Church. She was a fourth generation Canadian Black who lived in North Buxton, Ontario. Her great-grandfather, Abraham Shadd, an abolitionist of the free state of Pennsylvania, moved his Quaker-educated family to Canada after the Fugitive Slave Act of 1850. The North Buxton native has taught all eight grades of the elementary schools in Kent and Essex Counties. She has been involved in the church and community for many years serving as a Sunday School Teacher, church clerk and instructor of various religious courses. In 1967, she chaired the opening ceremonies for the Centennial opening of the Rawleigh Township Museum.

## HAZEL FORBES

Hazel Forbes was born in Toronto and has been the publicity director of the O'Keefe Centre for nineteen years. After studying at the Institute of Child Study, University of Toronto, she moved to New York where she helped found the Negro Digest. Forbes also spent a year working for the New China News Agency in London, England.

Her work at the O'Keefe Centre involved dealing with the media about features on performers and shows, releasing information, photographs, and often, escorting performers to radio and television interviews. As publicity director, she enjoyed meeting stars such as Pearl Bailey, Lena Horne, Miriam Makeba, Richard Burton and Elizabeth Taylor.

Hazel Forbes passed away in 1981.

## JENI LE GON

Actor, choreographer, dancer, once called 'Hollywood's Cinderella Girl,' Jeni Le Gon's remarkable career in show business has spanned nearly fifty years, beginning at thirteen when she made her first professional appearance dancing in a Broadway musical with the late Count Basie.

Le Gon, who grew up in southside Chicago during the Depression, knew from a young age that she wanted to be a dancer. But there wasn't any extra money around for lessons and she had to be content with learning dance steps from dancers on the screen.

She has lived in Vancouver, British Columbia for the past seventeen years where she is a choreographer. Her latest ventures includes 'Roots! and All That Jazz,' a revue that traces the influence of African heritage on the music and dancing of the Americas and the West Indies as well as the current blend of African and American Jazz.

## PAMELA APPELT

Pamela Appelt was appointed Citizenship Judge in 1987. A native of Jamaica, she began her adult life some twenty years ago as a biochemistry student at McGill University in Montreal. From there, she became increasingly interested in three-dimensional decoupage, a rare, 17th century art. (Decoupage is the art of creating three dimensions with paper cut-outs from two dimensional pictures.) Her unique pieces have been displayed worldwide. Appelt stresses the importance of preparing for more than one occupation in life. She is often invited to lecture and take part in ceremonies throughout Canada.

## DORIS FERGUSON

Doris Ferguson was born in Toronto of Caribbean parents. She has been involved in Black community organizations and activities for many years, dating back to the Home Service organization, Universal Negro Improvement Association and the Negro Choral Society. Doris was also a member of the St. Christopher House, University Settlement, and African Ensemble.

She has been involved in drama, appearing on Toronto Stage, CBC-TV and the National Film Board.
She was a member of the Ontario Black History Society and the Fuanga Club, a club assisting Ontario scholars.

In 1981, she was appointed Community Liaison counsellor, consulting with teachers, principals and guidance counsellors at both the elementary and secondary levels.

As Liaison Counsellor, Ferguson assisted parents, students and worked with organizations in the West Indian and Black communities.

She visited schools in Kingston and Montego Bay but did the majority of her research in Brown's Town, St. Ann which had a cross section of the different types of schools operating in Jamaica. Doris Ferguson retired from the Scarborough Board in June 1992.

## ALDA ARTHUR

Alda was born in Sydney, Nova Scotia, has resided in Toronto over twenty years and her occupations have been varied. After completing a Nursing Assistant's course she graduated from the Addiction Research Foundation as a Counsellor and worked there for seven years. Alda Arthur, a multi-talented woman of many interests was the founder and publisher of a business tabloid, Women and Business. The business folded in 1984. An interest dear to Alda's heart was the founding of the Association of Black Women in 1982: a club of Black business and professional women who provided support and information through business contacts and career development programs.

Arthur said that the Association of Black Women did not isolate themselves as a Black group, but shared their experiences with all women. The high-profile group improved their skills by attending seminars and workshops in the community as role models. Although the club folded in

1986 Arthur continued to meet challenges on a day to day basis and is always ready to move on to other opportunities. "My hope is that someday the Association will rise again, in another form, by spirited Black women. It's a need that should never die", she says with confidence.

## MARLENE GREEN

Originally from Dominica, Marlene Green have lived in Canada for over twenty-five years. She became active in the Toronto Black community through the Black Education Project in 1970. As Education Co-ordinator she worked both on co-ordinating the after-school programme and on community mobilization around issues that were of critical importance to the community, as they still are now; for example, racism in schools and police harassment of black youth.

The Black Education Project provided a training ground for many of us in the community. Within the project we volunteered as tutors, organized summer programmes, sponsored conferences, mobilized the community to support the struggles of African people all over the world, organized the African Liberation Support Committee which initiated observance of African Liberation Day. "I also worked in close collaboration with other community organizations like the UAIA, the Black Heritage Association, Harriet Tubman Centre, the Library of Black Peoples Literature and others too numerous to mention. For the ten years of its existence, the BEP provided leadership within the community and was a catalyst to other organizations.

In 1979, Green joined the staff of CUSO, an international, creative energies were being channelled into innovative approaches to changing the conditions of poverty and underdevelopment.

Illness bought Marlene Green back to Canada for a year, and on returning to work she was posted in Zambia as the Regional Director of CUSO's programmes in East, Central and Southern Africa. She was also responsible for managing programmes in Botswana, Mozambique, Tanzania, Zambia, Zimbabwe, a solidarity Liberation Support Programme with the ANC and SWAPO, and for initiating programmes in Angola and Namibia.

## THELMA CAREY THOMPSON

Born in Jamaica, Thelma Carey Thompson began to paint at the age of five. In 1952, she painted her first oil, an orchid in a pot. It was entered in the National Art Exhibition in Jamaica and was judged the best painting. Two years later, Carey Thompson went to London, England to study with Edward S. Annison. After her return to Jamaica, her portraits, landscapes and floral studies of tropical plants and flowers were sold through Hills Galleries and exhibited at the Institute of Jamaica and the Contemporary Jamaican Artist Association. She also joined the Jamaican Artist Guild.

In 1964, after the death of her husband, she immigrated to the United States where she attended the Albert Pels School of Art in New York City. In 1976, Thompson immigrated to Canada. She has held art shows at York University, Ryerson, and the John B. Aird Gallery.

## AMANDA JANET WARE

Amanda Janet 'Nettie' Ware was born in 1893 near Calgary, Alberta. Her father, known as the first Black cowboy, had been born into slavery. Her mother, the former Mildred Lewis, was the daughter of the first Black couple in that area.

Her mother maintained that learning to ride a horse was the ruination of a girl, but Ware learned to ride a horse almost as soon as she learned to walk. Friends remember her carrying cakes with icing to meetings while riding on horseback.

There were no schools in the area, so Ware was sent to live with her Grandmother Lewis to attend school, which proved to be a rather terrifying experience for her. Her mother and father both died in 1905.

Ware and her extended family moved back to Calgary in 1917. Her duties on the farm included milking cows and raising chickens. She was active in the Kirkcaldy Women's Institute for over fifty years.

The Ware family's log cabin was moved to a park site on the Red Deer River, Alberta in 1954. The cabin houses mementos of Ware's father and other local pioneers.

## JACKIE RICHARDSON TORONTO

Born in Pittsburg, Pennyslvania Jackie Richardson came to Canada at a young age and has been professionally involved in Canada's artistic community for over twenty years.

A multi-faceted entertainer, Jackie, at eight years of age, started out singing in the choir at the First Baptist Church on Huron Street in Toronto. From there, she joined with her girlfriends who formed an all-female group called Tiaras. Tiaras performed throughout Ontario playing the club circuit, which eventually landed them a half-hour television spot on show called Music Hop.

For Jackie, achieving a recognized position in the entertainment industry in Canada has not been easy. Like any form of freelance work, there were many roads and choices for her to take along the way. After doing background vocals for singers Diane Brooks and David Clayton Thomas, Jackie moved to Montreal and joined with an all female group called the Avalons. This was a short-lived venture for Jackie who then joined with the Platters embarking on a world tour that took the group to Hawaii, Tahiti, Fiji, New Zealand, Australia and Thailand where the group did a command performance for the Prince and Prime Minister of Thailand.

While still launching her musical career, Richardson began to involve herself in theatre - a career choice that would turn out to be very fruitful and rewarding for her in future years. She became a member of the North York Theatre of Performing Arts where she appeared as the character Pauline in 'No No Nanette'.

Although the road has been rough and rocky. Jackie has succeeded in making a name for herself in the entertainment business in Canada as well as abroad.

## BETTY RILEY

Canadian born Betty Riley was the first Black woman to produce a Black television series in Canada. She was founder and producer of "Black Is", a community program which was broadcast on cable television in Montreal during the 1970's.

The programs brought current news and events taking place in Montreal and abroad, special interest stories of various Black people from all parts of the world, and contemporary Black History, politics and culture.

Riley's family dates back to 1871, when slaves came to Canada from Sierra Leone, and settled in Nova Scotia.

She was a member of the National Black Coalition and executive director of the Black Community Media Inc., in Montreal. In 1974 she was honoured as one of the Black Women of the century at the Second National Congress of Black women in Montreal, 1974.

## ELIZABETH MARIA DUVAL ROLLING

From an early age, Elizabeth Rolling, born in 1877 to William and Maria Duval of Collingwood, was playing tunes by ear on the piano. Her aptitude developed to such an extent that even without formal training she was able to obtain employment with the Barrie Silent Movie Theatre. As an accompanist in the nickledeons of Silent Movie days Elizabeth Rolling had to provide the right background music for the scene depicted in the movie. Without words, the music set the mood and created the atmosphere for the acting.

Elizabeth Duval married William Rolling, a building contractor, and they moved shortly after marriage to Barrie, Ontario. There Mrs. Rolling set up a business as one of the leading dressmakers in the town, while still practising her music. It was in this musical environment that her only daughter, Vera was born and later grand-daughter, Phyllis Marshall and great grand-daughter Sharon.

Elizabeth Rolling was fortunate enough to see three generations reach successful maturity before she died in 1972. And up to a few months before her death she was still playing the Piano, a feat performed at her great grand-daughter's wedding.

## BEVERLEY SALMON

Beverley Salmon was the first Black Female Provincial Human Rights Commissioner. Born and raised in Toronto, her mother was a fifth generation Canadian of Scottish and Irish descent. Salmon's father came to Canada from Jamaica in 1917 to serve in the Canadian Army and later established a car repair business. Beverley Salmon graduated from the Wellesley Hospital School of Nursing and pursued post-graduate training in public Health Nursing at the University of Toronto. As a Public Health Nurse, she became sensitized to the needs of individuals of different ethno-cultural backgrounds. She founded the Toronto Urban Alliance on Race Relations and was an early supporter of the National Black Coalition of Canada. She was the founding chairperson of the Black Liason Committee of the Toronto Board of Education and has served on the Status of Women's Committee at the North York Board of Education. In 1985, Salmon was elected to the North York and Metro Councils, while also serving as an alderman. She has been married to Dr. Douglas Salmon for over thirty years and they have four grown children.

## MARY ANN SHADD

Mary Ann Shadd was born in 1823 in Wilmington, Delaware and came to Ontario in the mid-1800s via the Underground Railroad. Hers was a life of 'firsts' and 'onlies'. The stunning Black pioneer was one of the first women to lecture in public. She was the first Black woman to found and edit a weekly newspaper -'The Provincial Freeman,' which circulated through Toronto, Windsor and Chatham. Shadd was the only woman to be commissioned as a recruiting officer during the American Civil War. In her later years, she returned to the United States and became the first female law student at Howard University in Washington, beginning her legal career at the age of sixty. Mary Ann Shadd died June 5, 1893 at the age of seventy. Fortunately, her memory is kept alive thanks to the Mary Shadd School in Scarborough, Ontario which was built in 1986. The spirit of Shadd can be felt in the school motto - 'Free to be.'

## SHERONA HALL

Sherona Hall was born in Kingston, Jamaica, at the foot of Wareika Hill, one of the poor areas of Eastern Kingston a predominantly Rastafarian community in those days. As a child she witnessed the birth of reggae music, and sat among musical greats like Don Drummond, Roland Alfonso, Tommy McCook, and the great Count Ossie and his band, the Mystic Revelation of Rastafari. Growing up, she witnessed a lot of injustices, including police violence, racism, and poverty.

Being one of the few in her area to get a scholarship to high school, she became very active politically at 14 years, representing her entire community in various matters.

She was influenced by Marcus Garvey teachings at an early age and in the late 60's became involved in one of the first Black Power newspapers in Jamiaca, the "Abeng". Sherona also played table tennis island wide, was an actress with the Little Theatre, Jamaica, and a dancer with the Edinborough Dance Group.

Upon arrival in Canada, she became involved with the African Liberation Solidarity Committee. She was involved with many other community organizations, including the Black Workers Group, in 1977. She also founded the Committee Against the Deportation of Immigrant Women (CADIW) in 1977, which was at the forefront of organizing against the deportation of women from the Caribbean. She is an ongoing organizer of the March 8th Coalition; International Women's Day activities since 1978 and was a member of the Women's Coalition Against Racism and Police Violence after the shooting of Sophia Cook in Toronto. Hall was the community outreach co-ordinator for the Nelson Mandela visit to Toronto and escort to Winnie Mandela on her visit to Toronto.

Her recent work includes bringing public attention to the plight of Black Nurses in Ontario hospitals, with a special focus on the recent layoffs and firings at the Northwestern Hospital. She has made representations on changes to the Ontario Human Rights CommissionSherona Hall continues to be politically active in Toronto. She is co-founder of Black Women for Progress.

## ALMETA SPEAKS

Internationally acclaimed vocalist Almeta Speaks has made a tremendous contribution to music. Speaks, who was born in North Carolina, and has resided in Canada for over thirty years, has appeared on countless radio and T.V. shows since the seventies.

She has performed in concerts and clubs in major cities in Canada as well in Africa, Australia and parts of Europe. She sang accompanied by Orpheus Chamber Choir in Toronto in 1992 at a benefit concert for the Isaac Akande Scholarship Fund.

Almeta Speaks is presently working on two major projects. One is a four hour mini series for T.V. on the contributions of Blacks to the historical life of Canada. This series will feature four families from four regions of Canada, of significance to the Black experience.

The other project is a Black Arts Initiative which is an educational and employment concept for Black Canadians.

## LUCILLE MAY JOHNSON

Lucille May Johnson, a woman born in Jamaica, travelled to Canada several years ago and subsequently became a Canadian citizen. Always fiercely proud of her African heritage, she continuously attended the celebrated African Liberation Day events of the seventies in Toronto. At these events she came prepared with Jamaican type refreshments and foods much to the enjoyment of huge sections of the audience.

Lucille Johnson has the kind of "presence" that is usually found among royalty than among ordinary souls of a colonial past. On meeting Lucille Johnson it takes only a few minutes to realize that the extent of her self-respect and self-confidence runs very deep.

She came to be known affectionately as "Granny" not only by members of her own family, but by non-relatives as well. She is in fact not only a grandmother but a great grandmother. Her status as Granny among her family and friends approximates the role of the "Elder" in traditional African society, because of her wisdom, temperment, intelligence, and knowledge of the social conditions around her. She is 79 years old and lives in Toronto.

# WOMEN AND BLACK CHURCHES

Since the early 1800s, the church has been the most important institution in the Black community. It has provided spiritual guidance while also acting as a unifying force. The Church has also provided a forum for education in Black history, literature and womens' issues. While men have been the founders of the churches, women have always been actively involved and have recently been taking leadership positions.

## RACHEL HACKLEY

One such leader was Rachel Christina Earll Hackley who became a Deaconess in the African Methodist Church (AME). She was born on November 22, 1905 at Holland Centre, Ontario. In 1949, she directed the first Young Peoples' Convention which celebrated its fortieth year in 1989. Over the years, the group has become a very important part of the Canadian Conference of the junior AME churches. The Ladies' Aid Society was named the Rachel Hackley Ladies' Aid Society of Grant Church, an honour well deserved.

## ADDIE AYLESTOCK

Addie Aylestock became the first woman to be ordained in the BME Conference in 1952. She ministered in North Buxton, Windsor, Shaw Street BME and East York BME. She has received many tributes throughout her years of service. In 1984, the Ladies' League of Christ Church BME presented her with a plaque for her dedication and outstanding service. Aylestock was also featured in the Canadian National Film Board production called Older, Stronger, Wiser, produced and distributed by the Canadian National Film Board.

## E MARKHAM

urke Markham arrived in
ained as a Local Preacher
37 and appointed Assistant
, edited and published the
ME Church. She was also
e Ladies' League of Christ
Mental Health Association's
up was founded by Markham
m the West Indies.

## MADAM LEONA M. BREWTON

Madam Leona M. Brewton was another outstanding leader in the Black Church. She was born in Emerson, Ohio in 1883 and graduated from the Toronto Bible College in 1949. She served as the President of the Missionary Society at the First Baptist Church in Toronto. Brewton founded the famous Young Men's Bible Class which was also attended by young women. The students learned about the Bible while also studying Black history and literature.

## GRACE PRICE TROTMAN

Grace Price Trotman founded the Negro Youth Movement and was the President of the Young Peoples' Literary Society of the BME Church. Trotman also co-directed a camp for Black children, specializing in Black history. Most of all, she is remembered for her musical career including the production of six operettas, including the 'Pirates of Penzance' and 'H.M.S. Pinafore.' She conducted and performed in support of the War Victims' Fund, directing the Negro Choral Group at Varsity Arena and Eaton's Auditorium. Trotman was an outstanding member of the BME Church and her work as a Choir Leader was considered to be one of her greatest achievements. In 1975, she received the Outstanding Woman Award in honour of International Women's Year and 'Woman for a Better Canada Award' from the BME Church. She was awarded a plaque at a Testimonial Dinner in her honour in 1978. Grace Trotman was seventy-one years old when she passed away in 1985.

## URSILLA LOVELL CLARKE

The Church has also provided a forum for the discussion of women's issues. In 1974, Ursilla Lovell Clarke, a life-long member of the African Methodist Episcopal Church, was one of three representatives from Canada to attend the 'Consultation on Sexism' which was organized by the World Council of Churches. Such an event was clearly a big step forward for women.

## MARION CROWLEY NEWBY

Music has always been an important part of the life of Marion Crowley Newby, a sixth-generation Canadian. Over the years, she has been a church pianist, organist, choir director and music supervisor for elementary school. Newby has used her singing talent to minister to others in song. She has toured Canada, America, Australia and New Zealand and completed an album entitled 'Glorified.' The album which includes hymns and spirituals is an enduring legacy of Marian Crowley Newby, who passed away in 1971.

## RUBY PETERS

A faithful member of the St. George of the Martyrs Anglican Church, Peters came to Canada from Jamaica in 1914 and made her home a haven for many new immigrants.

Ruby Peters passed away in Toronto in 1984 at 90 years of age. She will always be remembered as being a friend to foreign students and was an active role model in the Black community.

## MARIAH RICHARDSON

Mariah Richardson was a life-long member of the British Methodist Church and was the mother of three children. She was an active member of the Household of Ruth Missionary Society of the B.M.E. Church, acting as Corresponding Secretary for this Association for twenty-four years.

Mrs. Richardson and her husband celebrated their golden wedding in 1966. She passed away in 1971. This Eulogy, one of many, was received in honour of Mariah Richardson's life:

> A king can make a noble man
> but only the 'Almighty' can
> make a person of virtue.

Mariah Richardson was honoured and recognized in the community for her wisdom and her understanding ways. Those who knew her were greatly strengthened and encouraged by her good deeds and her kindness. She was truly a humanitarian.

## VIOLA WATKINS

Viola Watkins was a co-founder of the Hour A Day Club and has held several positions in the organization. She served as secretary to the Emancipation Celebration Committee under the direction of Walter Perry, the promoter and held many offices in the Local Council of Women of Windsor. Watkins taught Sunday School for nearly ten years in St. Phillips Anglican Church.

From 1945-1963, Watkins was secretary to the Vocational Services Department of the Detroit, Michigan Urban League, a social work agency, and one of sixty two affiliates of the National Urban League. She also served as president of the Administrative and Clerical Council for two years, representing the administrative and clerical workers in sixty-two affiliates located throughout the United States.

Viola Watkins has pursued her profession, church, clubs and civic activities with perseverance, diligence and fortitude.

## EUNICE HYATT KERSEY

Eunice Kersey was born in Windsor, Ontario to a pioneer family which migrated to the area from Ohio in the early 1800's. Her father, who was a florist, was a very learned man who established one of Windsor's first Black businesses.

Mrs. Kersey was the area's second Black female school teacher and taught in the Windsor school system from 1917-1923.

Active in one of the local Black churches, she served as Sunday School Superintendent for many years and was the church historian, writing about most of the church activities for over thirty-five years.

She was active in several community organizations and was a Charter member of the Windsor Art and Literacy Club which was founded in 1924. Her mother, Laura Hyatt, was one of the co-founders of this club.

Eunice married George Kersey and they had four children and many grandchildren.

During World War II, Kersey worked as a volunteer with the Red Cross and was a founding member of the Cerebral Palsy Parent Association of Windsor and Essex County. She was appointed to the Mayor's task force in planning the famous Emancipation Day Celebrations.

In 1965, Kersey served on the committee of 'From Slavery to Freedom' Exhibition which was co-sponsored by the Toronto Black Business and Professional Men's Club and the University of Windsor. She was designated as one of the chief advisors for compiling and preparing the Exhibit at the University.

She passed away in 1966.

## AGATHA KING

Agatha King emigrated from Jamaica to Kempville, Ontario in 1929 and arrived in Toronto three years later. She was actively involved in church fundraising for the First Baptist Church for over 50 years. King was part of the delegation of prominent community activists who petitioned the Federal government on behalf of West Indian immigrants in the early years.

Agatha King passed away in 1982 at the age of 83.

## ODESSA SKEIR ARMSTRONG

Odessa Skeir Armstrong has worked as the secretary of the East York/ Scarborough B.M.E. Church, secretary of the Prince Hall Chapter of Eastern Star of Ontario, and recording secretary of the Elks of the World, Queen City Temple No. 1003. She has also worked as the secretary of the Good Will Club, a Black women's social club. Skeir has been the president of the Negro Credit Union and a member of the Catholic Children's Aide Foster Parents' Association. She has been associated with the Universal Negro Improvement Association and the Ontario Black History Society.

Halifax-born Odessa Skeir Armstrong has always had a special interest in politics. She has worked as an enumerator, a poll clerk and deputy returning officer. Skeir, who is retired from her work as a production coordinator with a large media corporation, has been an advocate for women and Blacks all her life.

## EDNA CARTER BRAITHWAITE

Born in 1896 in St. Phillips, Barbados, Edna Carter Braithwaite came to Canada in 1919, first to Nova Scotia and then settling in Montreal, Quebec. Braithwaite was active in the Salvation Army, the Negro Universal Improvement Association, the Negro Community Centre, Tyndale House and Welcome Hall Mission, which is still open.

Braithwaite met Marcus Garvey, the Jamaican-born founder of the UNIA on a visit to Montreal. She remembers buying shares in the Black Star Line which was also founded by Garvey.

Her first church was the Union United on Delisle Street in Montreal. Throughout the years, she has also attended St. George Anglican Church and evangelical churches.

## RETA DUVAL CUMMINGS

Reta Duval Cummings is a third-generation Canadian. Her parents, Charles and Edwina Duval settled in Collingwood in the late 1800s and operated an ice-cream parlour and barber shop in the area.

While living in Montreal from 1931 to 1954, Cummings became an active member of the Union United Church and the Coloured Women's Club. She is a life member of the Collingwood B.M.E. Community Heritage Church. In Toronto, where she frequently visits, she served as President of the Eureka Friendly Club.

Cummings is Associate Matron of the Ada Chapter No. 7, a Subordinate Chapter of the Eastern Star, and became an honourary member of the Ontario Black History Society at the 1986 Annual Meeting. An inspiration to all who meet her, Cummings looks forward to many more years of involvement.

## WOMEN'S ORGANIZATIONS

**B**lack womens' organizations have been absolutely crucial to the community. They have been dedicated to the advancement of Blacks in education, business and community service. The women have worked together, with and in support of one another. The motto of the Eureka Friendly Club, 'Not for ourselves, but for others,' reflects the spirit of each of the womens' groups.

### EUREKA FRIENDLY CLUB

The Eureka Friendly Club was founded in 1910 by a small group of women in Toronto. The club motto - 'Not for ourselves, but for others,' has motivated the women to do everything from assisting with rent and hospital bills, to delivering food baskets and awarding scholarships.

**Eureka Friendly Club, Charter Officers 1910**
Mrs. Perry-President
Mrs. Carter-Secretary
Mrs. Jackson-Treasurer

**Officers 1960**
Mrs. Redmon
Mrs. Carrington
Mrs. Darrell
Mrs. Marshall
Mrs. Fleming

**Members**
Mrs. Bradley
Mrs. Carter
Mrs. Deas
Mrs. Griffith
Mrs. Hackley
Mrs. Overton
Mrs. Parker
Mrs. Payne
Mrs. Perry
Mrs. Pittman
Mrs. Taylor
Mrs. Wilson

**Honourary Members**
Mrs. Brewton
Mrs. Crowley
Mrs. Daniel
Mrs. Mitchell
Mrs. E. Rolling

Photo Eureka Friendly Club- A group of early members
(Alphabetically named)
Bradley, Carter, Crowley, Darrell, Griffith, Marshall,
Martin, Meyers, Overton, Perry, Pittman

## THE COLOURED WOMEN'S CLUB

The Coloured Women's Club was founded in 1902 in Montreal by a group of women including the late Tilly Mays who lived to be one hundred and one years of age. Socially conscious women decided to help the soldiers who were returning from the Boer War. The club took care of the injured, organized soup kitchens, rolled bandages and provided temporary homes for the soldiers. The women also provided warm clothing for West Indian immigrants and welcomed them into the community. The women worked closely with the Union United Church in Montreal and provided books for the Black Studies library at the Negro Community Centre. At a membership drive, dinner-dance in 1977, club president Maisie Dickerson-Dash and Dr. Carrie Best of Halifax spoke on the role of Black women.

## THE HOUR A DAY STUDY CLUB

The Hour A Day Study Club, formerly the Mothers' Club, was founded in 1934 in Windsor, Ontario. The group organized at the home of Mrs. J.A. Jacobs, who became the first president, serving from 1934 to 1942. Under the motto, 'Working Together for Community Betterment,' the women contributed to the community through lectures, tours, home economics, current events and the study of Black history. During World War II, members performed clerical duties at the salvage depot, knitted for the Red Cross and awarded scholarships and bursaries. The club helped finance and coordinate Negro History Exhibits. The women participated in Windsor's Centennial in 1954 and in Canada's Centennial in 1967. One of the club's most memorable occasions was the hosting of the Fourth National Congress of Black Women in 1977. In celebration of the club's fiftieth anniversary in 1984, the women welcomed Shirley Chisholm, the first Black woman elected to the United States' Congress.

## THE CANADIAN NEGRO WOMEN'S ASSOCIATION (CANEWA)

The Canadian Negro Women's Association was founded in 1951 by Kay Livingstone, Aileen Williams, Audrey Grayson and Eugenee Ames. These women were dedicated to the advancement of Blacks in public education, business and community service. Internationally, the women have worked with UNESCO, raising funds to build a shelter in Ghana for Biafran children, while also donating money to the Toronto Committee for the Liberation of South Africa. CANEWA members, Enid D'Oylely and Rella Braithwaite recently published a book entitled Women of Our Times.

## SISTER VISION PRESS

Sister Vision Press, the first and only Canadian publishing house dedicated specifically to Black women and women of colour, was founded in 1985 by Makeda Silvera and Stephanie Martin. The press has provided a forum for women's issues, oral history, short stories, poetry, and writing for young people. The press is located in Toronto, Ontario.

## THE CONGRESS OF BLACK WOMEN

One of CANEWA's major achievements was the founding of the Congress of Black Women in 1973. A hard-working steering committee, including Kay Livingstone, Aileen Williams, Verda Cook and Eugenee Allen, organized committees and planned workshops for the three day event held in April, 1973. Over three hundred Black women met to discuss issues such as education, health and welfare, youth, immigration, the Black family, daycare services, human rights and racism. The resolutions passed later strengthened the bonds of communication between Black women of African, Caribbean, American and Canadian origin. In 1987, the Ontario Region of the Congress of Black Women presented the first annual Kay Livingstone Award to Jean Augustine. In May 1989, the North York chapter honoured three of its dedicated members, Sybil Garrick, Faye Cole and Catherine Howard. The Women of Our Times Award, designed by Donna Lee Bolden, was in keeping with the Congress' philosophy of women working together, and in support of each other. In June 1989, the Mississauga Chapter marked its first year by awarding scholarships of $500 each to Sonja Salmon, Cheryl Gibbons and Shuchanna Swawby.

## EARLY BLACK WOMEN'S CLUBS IN EASTERN CANADA

In the early years of free Black settlement in Canada, there were many needs to meet. In 1840, Ellen Toyer Abbott founded the Queen Victoria Benevolent Society which offered aid to the poor.

Women of the Well, a church group, formed in 1914 was organized in Halifax and helped to raise funds to establish a normal and industrial school. In the 1920s, a group of women formed the Little Mother's League in Montreal. These groups aimed to make 'little Negro girls proficient in household duties.' This was quite an achievement in the 1920s.

In 1919, the Women's Charitable Benevolent Association was founded in Montreal. The women's activities included operating soup kitchens and rolling bandages for the Red Cross.

Montreal's Phyllis Wheatley Club, named after the early poet, was founded by Lillian Rutherford in 1922. The cultural club became the Negro Theatre Guild of Montreal in the mid-1930s.

Early Black Canadian women generally worked as domestics, maids and cleaners for the well-to-do, but they continued to be involved in their churches and community. The early Black Lodges have always had women's groups and the Toronto Negro Colour Guard Ladies' Auxiliary was an active group.

# THE EARLY BLACK CHURCH

The history of the Black Church in Canada goes back to the early 1800s when the most important institution in all Black communities was the church. Religion played a very important role.

The early churches including the British Methodist Episcopal, the African Methodist Episcopal and the First Baptist Church were the main Black churches in Ontario for over 160 years, after serving four generations. Of most historic signifance to present day Black Nova Scotians is the African Baptist Church.

The more recent West Indian communities have made considerable contributions to the churches and have founded numerous churches in Canada.

The African Methodist members are constantly reminded of Richard Allen. He was a former slave who had bought his freedom and was a member of Philadelphia's St. George Methodist Church in 1787 where he experienced discrimination.

At that time, Blacks were relegated to certain pews, but Allen and other Blacks were often forced out of the church. Allen and his supporters founded the Free African Society and other AME churches where Blacks could worship.

In 1816, the churches united to form the AME Church, and Allen became its first Bishop.

Beginning in the 1820's, Black refugees entering Canada formed their own congregations and since most American Blacks had belonged to Methodist or Baptist groups, they were eager to belong to similar denominations. Churches were the strength of the Black communities.

Around the year 1834, African Methodist Episcopal ministers of the United States came to Canada and preached to Black settlers of Methodist religion. They formed Societies and organized an Annual Conference, known as the Canadian Annual Conference.

After a few AME Churches and congregations were founded in Canada, it was found to be inconvenient to be under a foreign Bishop and discipline. There was a division between the churches and some members wished to replace the American connection with a British name.

In 1856, the Canadian Annual Conference meeting was held in Chatham. Members of the conference decided to form a separate independent church to be known as the British Methodist Episcopal Church with Bishop Willis Nazrey appointed as the BME church's first Bishop.

Toronto's first BME Church was built in 1884 at 92 Chestnut Street by the Black community. Another building which was later built on Chestnut Street was sold to a congregation during the 1950's and for many years, held the Chinese United Church.

During 1949, the BME conference, under the leadership of General Superintendent Jackson, held union discussions with the Afro-Community Church which was situated on Elm Street. Many Torontonians remember attending the special gatherings held at the Elm Street Church.

Rev. Dr. Cecil Stewart, the Pastor, with Rev. Dr. Markham, Assistant Pastor and congregation agreed to unite the BME and Afro-Community Church. Through this union in 1951, the BME was able to acquire their present site. Christ Church BME is located on Shaw Street.

## GRANT AME CHURCH

The Toronto Grant AME Episcopal was named after Bishop Abraham Grant. It was built on Richmond Street East of York in 1833. After 1912, the congregation met at a hall on University Avenue where the Sick Children's Hospital now stands. In 1929, it moved to Soho Street. In 1988, the AME Church on Soho Street was sold. Its present site is 2029 Gerrard Street East. The pastor of the church is Rev. Parker.

## FIRST BAPTIST CHURCH

Ontario's oldest Baptist congregation was founded by a group of twelve slaves who had come to Canada via the famous Underground Railway in the early 1800's.

Elder Washington from Virginia, USA arrived in Canada in 1825 to serve refugee slaves. He organized the First Baptist Church in 1826 and served as pastor until his death in 1850.

After meeting in private homes and in a schoolhouse, the first Baptist Church was build at the corner of Victoria and Queen Street in 1841. This property was sold in 1905. A new building was constructed at the corner of University and Edward Street. In 1955, the present location at 101 Huron Street was built under the chairmanship of the late Dr. O. Brewton.

The popular spiritual guidance church at 101 Huron Street has been pastored by Rev. Eustace Mead since 1976.

# EAST YORK SCARBOROUGH BME CHURCH

After Toronto's BME Church had been active for over one hundred years, it was realized that many of its congregation had moved to suburban areas. The Rev. Dr. Markham was approached regarding opening a church closer to the members. Arrangements were made with Westview Presbyterian Church. The East\York Scarborough BME Church was founded in 1978 and has been able to hold their services in this church.

In July, 1979 at the 123rd Annual Conference held in London, Ontario, the church became a member of the conference. Bishop Markham assisted by Rev. O. Rupwate, became the first pastors followed by Rev. Livingstone Yearwood. The late Rev. Keith Blackburn was given charge of the church in 1984. After ministering to this church for four years, he passed away in 1988.

Rev. Addie Aylestock pastored the church until Conference time when Rev. Dr. Arthur May was installed in July, 1988. That same year, the East York\Scarborough Church celebrated its first ten years. To date, the Church is still meeting at Westview Presbyterian Church on 233 Westview Blvd. They hope to have a building of their own in the near future.

# THE BLACK MEDIA

## THE EARLY BLACK PRESS IN CANADA

The first Black paper, the *Voice of the Fugitive*, was published bi-monthly by Henry Bibb in Sandwich and Windsor, Ontario between 1851 and 1857.

The next successful paper, the *Provincial Freeman*, founded by Samuel Ward, was launched in Windsor, Ontario in 1853. The next year it was produced in Toronto, and then Chatham, Ontario. It carried anti-slavery news and was later edited by a Black woman, Mary Ann Shadd, who was an early women's rights activist.

She lectured and addressed public gatherings at a time when women hardly dared to speak in public and was acknowledged as the first Black newspaper woman in North America.

Shadd carried her views on abolition of slavery and her editorials urged Blacks to settle in Canada with a view to permanency, not to have one foot in Canada and the other foot in the United States.

The early papers stressed equality and opportunities for Blacks via different methods. Henry Bibb was in favour of organizing refuge communities while Mary Ann Shadd urged the Blacks to be more independent, self-supporting and to strike out on their own.

The third pioneer paper, the *British Lion*, 1881 to 1912, appeared in Hamilton. The most intellectual paper was the Neith, a monthly, edited by A.B. Walker, a lawyer and a journalist for a short time in Saint John, New Brunswick in 1903.

Walker was born in British Columbia, studied law in the United States and toured the South giving lectures. His magazine promoted brotherhood between all peoples. He was said to believe in colonization in Africa, where Canadian, West Indians and American Blacks would live under British rule in an interracial colony of their own. He opposed Washington's industrial training program.

*The Dawn of Tomorrow* was edited and published by James Jenkins in London, Ontario from 1923-1931, the time of his death. His widow, Christine Jenkins assumed editorial responsibilities and strived to build up the circulation when the newspaper almost ceased to exist in 1939. By 1950, the *Dawn of Tomorrow* enjoyed a circulation in many countries beyond Canada and today a limited amount of copies are still produced in London by some of the family.

Following World War II, a tabloid called *the Clarion* was published in Nova Scotia by a human rights activist, a distinguished writer and lecturer, Dr. Carrie Best. The Clarion was dedicated to the improvement of racial relations and it was the only paper written exclusively for Blacks in the Maritimes. Carrie tested areas in regards to the degree of discrimination, then wrote about those areas.

In Toronto, the *Canadian Negro Paper* was issued weekly from 1953 to 1956. It was edited by Roy Greenridge and Donald Carty. Later, John White, brother of the late singer, Portia White and William White, took over as editor and Danny Braithwaite also wrote for the Canadian Negro.

*Africa Speaks*, a monthly paper, was published in Toronto by the late Carl Woodbeck. This paper, founded in the fifties, was later published periodically until the early seventies. The very small tabloid which later became a larger size, carried mostly advertising as well as descriptive columns which Woodbeck had researched on the businesses. The paper also carried social columns written by correspondents from Owen Sound and St. Catherines, where there were still a few Black families and Black Churches. From 1971 to 1974, Rella Braithwaite wrote a column for *Africa Speaks*.

Carl Woodbeck used profits from the paper for Black student scholarships. He was killed in a car accident in Buffalo in 1978. The paper was no longer published.

## RECENT PUBLICATIONS

In more recent years, Toronto has been the base of many papers and magazines. In 1972, a new quarterly magazine, *Black Images* was published in Toronto. *Spear*, a well designed magazine with correspondents in the United States, the Caribbean and Africa, also started publication in 1972. *Spear* was a black magazine that spoke to the issue of the time, and to young blacks who were influenced by the Black Power Movement south of the border. It was a magazine that inspired blacks to write and express themselves. Publisher/Editor Danny Gooding, struggled with the magazine for many years. *Spear* closed its door in 1981.

In the mid seventies, *Talking Drums*, an eight and a half inch weekly magazine was founded by Publisher/Editor Duke Vanderpuije, an African immigrant. The magazine later became a bi-monthly, but folded shortly due to the death of the publisher.

*Pride Magazine*, a Black/Caribbean weekly with a circulation of 25,000 was founded by Publisher/ Editor Michael Van Cooten. *Pride* aims to reflect the ambitions, aspirations, achievements of the Canadian Blacks and West Indian community.

One of the most recent magazines to be published in Toronto was Excellence, launched in 1986 by Arnold Augustine, Publisher of *Share Newspaper*. The women's magazine had strong positive images and was definitely a benefit to the community. With Managing Editor, Sandra Whitting and other qualified staff, the magazine with the attractive glossy cover was well received until its last issue in the summer of 1988.

*Our Lives* - Canada's First Black Women's Magazine was founded by a collective group of enlightened, concerned young Black women in 1986. The paper stressed women's problems and resolutions. The paper folded after a short life.

## SHARE PUBLICATIONS

Share, is a highly respected Black newspaper which strives to reflect Black and West Indian successes and goals. The paper was founded in January 1978 by Trinidadian-born Arnold A. Auguste. He and his managing editor, Jules Elder vowed to make the readers proud by sharing the news of Blacks and West Indians and their accomplishments, while also sharing the sadness of those in trouble.

After fourteen years in service, Share still continues to strive for excellence. Arnold and his committed staff put special emphasis on positive news.

Share has an estimated readership of over 75,000, making it the largest ethnic newspaper. The publication has received over twenty awards. Auguste, along with other press publishers, was honoured during media week in 1985 by the Toronto Press Club at an event sponsored by the Canadian Ethnic Journalists and Writers Club (CEJW).

In 1988, North York Mayor Tonks paid tribute to Share for ten years of professional journalism and cited the papers' policy of focusing on the positive aspects of the Black and West Indian community.

Share depends solely on advertising, does not accept government grants and is one hundred percent Black and West Indian owned. The publication, which includes a great deal of Caribbean and African news, serves a much needed service to Blacks and the wider community.

## ISLANDER PUBLICATIONS

The Islander was founded in 1973 in Toronto by Bromley Armstrong, a Black activist who felt it necessary to better inform the large West Indian Community of developments in their respective homelands as well as in their new environment.

Despite the presence of Contrast, which had been published by Al Hamilton since 1969, The Islander went from a twice-monthly newspaper to a successful weekly. After four years, however, in 1977, Armstrong and Hamilton merged the two publications to produce a more dynamic newspaper with all the Caribbean news carried in one section of Contrast, entitled The Islander. The two publishers were commended for taking such a giant step.

During the four years of publications, The Islander annually held a successful anniversary award dinner where, the paper would award outstanding Black individuals. In 1975, five involved persons, Dr. George Bancroft, Esther Hayes, Austin Clarke and the late Rt. Rev. Dr. Markham and Tom Sosa received awards. Hon. Margaret Birch, Provincial Secretary for Social Development at that time, was the Guest Speaker.

## CONTRAST PUBLICATIONS

Contrast was founded in Toronto in 1969 by Al Hamilton, an advertising salesman. Contrast's first headquarters was on Lennox Street in the Bloor and Bathurst area.

Edmonton-born Hamilton, whose grandparents came to Canada in 1909, saw the need for a paper written for Blacks by Blacks. Contrast started out as a bi-monthly and was edited by Olivia Grange Walker, now a Jamaican Senator and journalist. Elizabeth Escobar, a fifth generation Canadian, also helped to get Contrast published and later became editor.

The very first issue of Contrast carried the confrontation between Black students and faculty at the Sir George Williams University, Montreal that led to the arrest and conviction of several Black students.

The paper soon became a weekly and in 1974, Contrast became a member of the National Newspaper Publishers Association in Washington, D.C. This enabled the paper to gain access to wider and a more complete coverage of North American affairs that affected the Black community.

Under the guidance of Hamilton and staff, the paper showed a sensitivity to the community's interests, and sponsored the first conference on the history of Blacks in Toronto.

In 1973, Contrast founded the Junior Achievement Awards for Black Youths, which were annually held in the form of a dinner for six years. It was an opportunity for the community to become acquainted with the high calibre of talent and academic involvement of the youth.

In this venture, Hamilton received the support of many Blacks in the community and notable persons such as Rosemary Brown and Gwen and Lennie Johnston of Third World Books. However, it proved to be an expensive venture and could not be continued after six years.

Throughout the years, the paper provided a forum for new journalists. Today, Black publishing is still a struggle, but not as much as it formerly was.

In February, 1989, Contrast's twentieth anniversary was officially recognised by the Minister of State for Multiculturalism, Gerry Weiner at a ceremony held in at Cable 47 (MTV). Unfortunately, Contrast closed its doors in February, 1991. Former editor, Lorna Simms with Associates went on to launch a new publication, *The Dawn Newspaper.*

Quite a number of our Black newspapers came on the market. During the early 1990's *The Dawn Newspaper* was established. The publication covers local news, sports and events throughout the community. It aims to give a positive reflection of the Black community.

Another paper which was also established in 1991, is *The Metro Word*, Toronto Black Culture Magazine which is published by Phillip Vassell. The paper covers the entertainment\literary and cultural happenings around the city. It also features in depth interviews with Blacks in various key positions in government, theatre, community work and music. *Ember* was published and edited by Katherine Walker Alleyne and Archibalo Alleyne in celebration of Black Women in Canada. One or two issues were published in 1991, but died shortly. This is not surprising given that the country's recession and the difficulty that Black publishers face.

There have been quite a number of other newspapers, not mentioned, that have sprung up in Toronto, and across the country. The challenge is always to keep them alive.

*Contrast* was published with any help Hamilton could find. Many contributors were volunteers. In 1972, Harold Hoyte, a journalist from Barbados, served as editor until he returned to his homeland. The same year, Austin Clark wrote a series of columns for the paper and was joined by a young African journalist, Jo Jo Chintoh, who is today a popular reporter at City TV. Hamilton Grange, a Toronto Star reporter, started his early years at *Contrast*.

Trinidad-born Daryl Dean and *Share* publisher Arnold Augustine, both served in the life of *Contrast*. Errol Townshend, a Metro lawyer worked as an Editorial Consultant for a time. Lennox Johnson, now editor of *The Sunday Express* in Trinidad and Tobago also worked for the publication.

Radicals sometimes complained that the paper was irrelevant to the real issues of Black oppression in Canada and moderates complained that the publication was too outspoken and radical. From the beginning, Hamilton remained dedicated and often admitted the paper was his whole life and a twenty-four hour a day job.

By 1982, *Contrast* had a circulation of 57,000. In 1983, Hamilton received a Canadian flag which once flew from the Peace Tower. It was from former Prime Minister Trudeay for fourteen years of outstanding service to the Black community. That same year, Hamilton sold Contrast to businessman Denham Jolly. He saw the need for communication in the Black community and when advertising and financial support was not sufficient from Toronto Blacks, he accepted advertising from places such as Montreal, Halifax, and Hamilton. The paper also carried profiles and news from those areas. In 1985, Jolly sold *Contrast* to publisher Horace Gooden.

*Contrast* held its first annual Contrast Canadian Black Achievement Awards at the Ryerson Theatre auditorium on October 1, 1988.

Publishing houses for books, by and about Black people, or women in particular have not been that many, and they have not had long lives. Reasons are most often due to lack of money for publishing and burn-out, because of the strenuous work load, the long hours, and the very little financial rewards.

*Williams-Wallace Publishers*, was founded by Ann Wallace and Jeffrey Pollard in 1979. Williams Wallace publishers produce and publish works by both Black men and women with an emphasis on literary work. To date, the company has a list of Black writers, Latin-American writers and works of writers from other immigrant communities.

*Sister Vision Press* is the first and only Black Women and Women of Colour publishing house to be established in Canada. It was founded by Makeda Silvera and Stephanie Martin in 1985. The press publish books that deal with issues of concern to women of colour. Books focus on women's oral history, novels, short stories, poetry, theory and research, and writings for children and young people. The press has served as a forum for many women who are writing in isolation. Through writing workshops and readings, women of colour are finding voices.

## EARLY BLACK ORGANIZATIONS

The Black community has many outstanding organizations that should be celebrated. The following groups are not solely women's organizations. They are included in this book because they are important to Black heritage. It is hoped that the reader will become involved in the community and learn more about Black history by visiting these organizations.

### THE ONTARIO BLACK HISTORY SOCIETY

The Ontario Black History Society, a registered charitable organization, was founded June 6, 1978 in Toronto by a small group of dedicated individuals, headed by Dr. Dan Hill.

Dan Hill, historian and author had long had a dream - to create the first Black History Society in this country. The first executive officers were Dan Hill, Wilson Brooks, Joan Kaczmarski, Lorraine Hubbard and Donna Hill.

Throughout the early years, many Canadian groups had met to discuss and study Black's history but this was the first time a Black History Society had been formed. The time had come. Blacks were realizing the importance of their heritage.

In the beginning the OBHS was involved with the Multicultural History Society of Ontario. A cooperative program between the two groups began with the OBHS staff and members receiving training on conducting interviews with senior members of the Black community.

Tapes, documents and other historical information were housed at the Archives of Ontario throughout the agency of the MHSO, as copies of this material were also kept at OBHS. This project was funded by the MHSO.

Lorraine Hubbard, who had leadership qualities, accepted the position of the first executive-director and project coordinator and was soon conducting oral history workshops which enabled members to obtain this precious information. She was very efficient in setting up exhibits and presentations in schools and libraries.

One of the first activities of the OBHS was to celebrate Black History Week in February, 1979. This occasion was well publicized in order for the city of Toronto and its Black community to have access to Black's history. The society under Hill's urging promoted the hanging and unveiling of a portrait of William Hubbard, an early Black politician in what was then known as new City Hall. In September 1979, a plaque was unveiled at Hubbard's former residence on Broadview Avenue.

In February 1981, the society teamed up with the Market Gallery archives' staff and mounted a very informative exhibition which was attended by over one thousand people. This function was funded by the Atkinson Charitable Foundation, the MHSO, the Department of Secretary of State and Wintario and was on display until March, 1981. Lorraine and Pam Wachna of the Market Gallery conducted eight private tours as well as nearly one hundred classroom tours.

In 1982, the society set up its own offices at 352 Sheppard Avenue East due to the generous support of Mr. Tom Stevens, paediatrician. By this time, the Public Education Program had become quite active as Black History videos and literature were distributed in schools, libraries, universities as well as to members.

Members and non-members were often invited to participate in OBHS projects and this factor captured larger audiences, as the OBHS progressed.

In 1983, Dan Hill was appointed Ontario Ombudsman. Members Paul Anderson and Rella Braithwaite co-chaired the society for two terms. Rella later stepped down and Paul was elected as president.

An honourary position of Founder and President Emeritus was created for Dan Hill, who remained involved in the OBHS. The remaining members of the 1983 board were Lorraine Hubbard, Sydney Blackwood, Vivian Chavis, Margaret Crawford and Robert Longworth.

In 1984, the society cooperated with the Bicentennial Black Heritage Celebration Committee in producing a presentation entitled Hallelujah Ontario. This theatrical production traced the two hundred year-old history of Black's contributions to Ontario.

On August 24, 1987 the OBHS moved to its new home at the Ontario Heritage Centre at 10 Adelaide Street in downtown Toronto. The Centre had been purchased by the Ontario Heritage Foundation, an agency of the Ministry of Culture and communication.

The society was happy to mark its tenth anniversary as one of the most exciting cultural and educational organizations when it held Freedom Fest at Toronto's Harbourfront in July, 1988. This enjoyable event, due to the cooperation of so many people, was attended by thousands. It was truly a festival of Black culture and heritage with high-profile performers enjoying a weekend of exhibits, entertainment and educational activities.

## BLACK LANDMARKS, SITES

### UNCLE TOM'S CABIN

The annual meetings are held in the fall in the form of a brunch at which time workshops and guest speakers are featured. At the 1988 annual meeting, several ten-year members received scrolls.

In 1988, the society co-sponsored the A Space gallery film program, Perspective on Film, which featured evening films and children's matinee. A successful Storytelling Brunch is held annually which is educational and entertaining.

The OBHS Newsletter including local and other material is mailed to members several times a year.

Dr. Dan Hill, founder of the Ontario Black History Society and author of The Freedom Seekers. Dr. Hill was the Ontario Ombudsman and the first Director of the Ontario Human Rights Commission.

If you're driving through northwestern Ontario, not far from Chatham, you might find yourself in a sleepy town called Dresden. If you have the time to explore the place, do, for it is a town with an interesting past. Stop by one dwelling in particular- Uncle Tom's Cabin, the former residence of a man upon whom Harriet Beecher Stowe based her powerful novel.

The real 'Uncle Tom' was a Reverend called Josiah Henson. He was born a slave in Maryland in 1789. In 1830, he escaped to Canada and freedom. In 1841, a decade before Dresden was formed, Henson and a group of abolitionists, bought 200 acres of land for $4 an acre. There, they established a vocational school which was known as the British Institute for fugitive slaves.

The cabin itself, which boasts a plaque outlining its history, is a simple structure of tulip wood siding held together by hand-made square nails. It was built in 1842 and still has a few of the original furnishings- bedroom furniture, a rocking chair, and a few of Josiah Henson's other possessions. The residence is now an official museum.

Other structure on the property include an agricultural building; a smoke house used to cure meat, a church (which originally stood elsewhere) that houses the pulpit from which Henson preached, and a former slave house- one of the first structures in the region where a fugitive slave could live in freedom.

Henson lived to the age of 93, and he and his family were buried in the cemetery facing the church.

## NORTH BUXTON AND RAWLEIGH TOWNSHIP MUSEUM

In 1993, the Elgin Settlement will celebrate its 143rd anniversary. The historical Black settlement was created under the guidance and supervision of Reverend William King in 1850. He acquired fifteen slaves from Louisiana and brought them to North Buxton School. By 1867, approximately two thousand people had settled there. The Buxton Mission became the first school in the area. By 1873, slaves were being set free and it appeared that the Elgin Association would no longer be needed. In 1967, the North Buxton Museum was officially opened as a Rawleigh Township Centennial Project and has become an important Black History Centre. North Buxton, which was once part of the Elgin Settlement, has become a historic meeting place. It has hosted annual Labour Day Homecomings were early settlers, friends and tourists from Canada and the United States join together in a celebration of Black culture.

## THE NORTH AMERICAN BLACK MUSEUM AND CULTURAL CENTRE

Amherstburg, Ontario might be another nondescript small town on the border if it weren't the home of the North American Black History Museum (NABHM). A sign at the city says 'It will be the pride of generations in brick and mortar' and in eight years since it was erected, this has proven true. It is located at 277 King Street.

The idea of a black museum and cultural centre in Amherstburg first surfaced about 25 years ago. The force behind it was a man called Melvin Simpson. He had concerns about the level of black awareness in his community. He felt that a stronger sense of awareness and pride in blacks would result from the creation of a central area that could honour the legacy of our black forefathers.

With this in mind, Simpson set himself to the task of raising funds. From 1964 until his death in 1982, the late Melvin Simpson and his family endeavoured to achieve his dream.

In recognition of this remarkable achievement and to honour the Museum's founder, the Amherstburg Chamber of Commerce named Mr. and Mrs. Simpson 'Citizen of the Year' in 1982. The award was accepted by Betty Simpson on behalf of her husband who died earlier that year.

But Simpson had lived long enough to see his life's work realized in the creation of a museum. More than a museum, the North American Black History Museum is a constant reminder of our origins in the great civilizations of Africa, the period of slavery and the successful struggle our ancestors endured for the freedom we enjoy today.

Today Amherstburg and North America are proud of the modern Black Historical Museum and restored log house to the period of 1855. The Nazery A.M.E. Chuch, phase three is being made into a Shrine in memory of all slaves who came to Canada hoping for a better way of life. A large board of directors, the Black community, the Nazery A.M.E. Church as well as the town of Amherstburg and the first province of Ontario have made this dream of Melvin and Betty Simpson's come true.

## BLACK THEATRE CANADA

Once squeezed between a cleaning store and a coin laundry, above a hairdressing shop on Vaughan Road in Toronto, Black Theatre Canada, a professional theatre, struggled to survive.

BTC was born out of a desire for change. In 1972 Vera Cudjoe, the company's founder and administrative/artistic director, set out to right some of the wrongs she felt were inherent in Canada theatre.

Employment opportunities for Black actors in Toronto during the late 70's were few and far between. The number of plays produced that were written by Blacks was small. Smaller still was the number of major roles requiring the casting of Black actors. Cudjoe, like many other Black actors working in Toronto at the time, had a career checkered with occasional small roles, non-acting jobs, and much unemployment. It was a sorry situation that Cudjoe endeavoured to repair.

"Black people are very much a part of the cultural institution of Canada," Cudjoe said. "And we hope to impress upon the people, the many contributions that Black people have made to the growth and development of Canada". With the energy and struggle Cudjoe invested in BTC, she counted herself among those notable contributors.

IN 1973 BTC's board included novelist Austin Clark, choreographer Len Gibson and past Alderman Ying Hope, along with other noted members.

The Theatre which ran its first series of youth workshops in the summer of 1973, rented offices from the City of Toronto at 13 Madison Avenue. Professional instructors such as the Jeff Henry, actor and professor at York University, Daniel Caudeiron, the director and associate producer of "Black World", and Len Gibson, founder-director of his own school, were the early workshop instructors.

These workshops employed Black youth in a theatre-training environment, in acting, dancing, voice, and studied the work of Black writers, poets and playwrights. Many of these young people, including Playwright Diana Braithwaite, pursued careers in acting, writing and music.

Dominican-born Amah Harris, a theatre major joined BTC during 1974 as co-director and assistant publicity-manager, and concentrated on children's workshops. She wrote a series of plays based on Anansi African folktales which were performed and well received in over seventy-five Metro elementary schools.

In 1978 Harris worked as artistic and executive director. She produced several productions while Cudjoe was away on a sabbatical leave. Harris later resigned and later worked on a freelance basis with the company.

In 1981 Robin Breon, a very dedicated assistant administrator and public relations officer, joined BTC and worked with Vera until the company closed. Breon tried to develop and encourage Black playwrights to pursue writing as a full time career.

Success greeted the young company to a large extent, but it has not been an easy road to hoe. Encouragement had been slow in coming and financial worries always hovered over the Black Theatre Canada dark storm cloud. In 1981, lack of funds forced the opening day cancellation of "Our Heroes," a play about Black Canadians.

Among the early productions of the 1970's were Stagolee in 1974 at Harbourfront. Layers and changes, with Delroy Linda and Gloria Sauve, who later went on to Broadway productions. Schools Out by Trevor Rhone and several other successes.

A Caribbean Midsummer Night's Dream, performed in 1983, was probably the most unusual setting in which Blacks would be seen. The play gave the Black actors an opportunity to perform in mainstream theatre. The production received rave reviews.

During the BTC's last two year period from 1986-1987 the company produced some of its most successful projects such as One More Stop on the Freedom Train but due to refusal of government funding the Black People's/Cultural Centre (which Black Theatre had incorporated in recent years), closed its doors in 1988.

## QUEBEC NAMES STREET AFTER JAMES E. DAVIS
## GREENFIELD PARK

On October 17, 1987 a former Greenfield Park, Quebec, resident, the late James E. Davis was immortalized when Mayor Stephen Olynyk and members of the city council unveiled a new street sign in his memory. The street which runs off Victoria Avenue was formerly known as Third Street but is now James E. Davis Street.

The ceremony attended by the council members, their wives and the Davis descendants was followed by a private civic reception in the Town Hall. Three generations of the Davis descendants including sons, daughters, grandchildren and great grandchildren participated in the historical event.

Born December 26, 1891 in St. Vincent, West Indies, Davis spend his early years working on his father's farm. In his early twenties, he emigrated to Great Britain where he joined the Merchant Marines and served on the H.M.S. Eaglet. He was honorably discharged in April 1920. In 1922 he married Gladys Irene Humphrey of Cardiff, Wales. Shortly after the couple emigrated to Canada, settling in Montreal where they had five children. At the time, Davis was employed by Redpath Sugar and remained with the company for twenty-five years.

In 1935 Davis and family moved to Greenfield Park where he had purchased a home and three acres of land. A few years later he purchased four more acres to expand his small farm, which he maintained while continuing his full time employment at Redpath Sugar.

The farm was active until 1960, but because of a housing boom in the area, Davis disposed of the livestock and farm. He passed away on September 24, 1972. His wife died six years later. Two of their children still reside in Greenfield Park.

He was honoured not only because his enterprising hard labour contributed greatly to the community, but because his family was the first Black family to live in this suburban town.

## BLACK CULTURAL CENTRE

The Black Cultural Centre of Nova Scotia opened in September, 1983. The centre was built by the Black Cultural Society in an effort to preserve Black culture in Nova Scotia. It consists of a library, archives, a museum and a small theatre. The museum has several artifacts, including 55 photographs documenting the history of Blacks in Nova Scotia after 1900 and before 1920. In addition to the permanent tributes, the centre houses many exhibits of Black artists, playwrights and military heroes. Gus Wedderburn, the Society's first president, pointed out that the 35,000 Loyalists who settled in Nova Scotia in 1782, about 4,000 were Blacks. The War of 1812 brought some 5,000 Black refugees from the United States.

## CARIBANA

For a few brief days every summer, the streets of Toronto are transported across the ocean to a group of islands, known collectively as the 'Caribbean.' And as the spirit of Caribana settles on the city, the Caribbean and African communities gather together to celebrate their culture.

In Canada, Caribana started in 1967 when the Caribbean Cultural Committee developed the project as a contribution to Canada's Centennial Celebration. Dr. J.A. Liverpool was the Chairman of the Caribana Committee.

Caribana is an extravaganza that has become traditional in Toronto and the highlight is the carnival parade that traverses the downtown in a blaze of colour and flair. It represents a culmination of several weeks of feverish preparation of floats and costumes. The mass parade has been a Caribbean custom since about 1783, when French settlers moved to Trinidad in large numbers to run plantations. During these early years, mass was very much an elite tradition.

Caribana, which has become an artistic expression of Toronto's Black community, has entrenched itself into the multicultural fabric of Toronto and many other Canadian cities, and is enjoyed by a wide cross-section of racial groups.

In 1992, the festival's 25th anniversary, more than 1000,000 spectators gathered to watch the parade. That made it not only the largest Caribana parade, but the biggest of any street parade ever held in Metro Toronto. But the parade is only part of the Festival.
Caribana is a salute to the food, music, crafts, dance and lifestyles of the West Indies. It is a gathering of common interests and connected lives. It is a group of people who join together for love of a distant land in a collective effort to bring it a little closer to home.

The province of Ontario, Metro Council, the City of Toronto as well as a contribution from Metro Toronto, representing all cities in the greater Toronto area, assist with funding.

Blacks are still questioning whether the Black and Caribbean community are actually benefitting from Caribana, as few Black businesses are in the parade route and it is imperative that the tourist patronize the local Caribbean restaurants, food and clothing stores, craft houses and book stores during the event.

Toronto's Caribana has generated interest to the extent that several Canadian cities hold a mini-Caribbean celebration after consultation with Caribana officials.

## MONTREAL BLACK COMMUNITY YOUTH CHOIR AND JUBILATION GOSPEL CHOIR

In 1974, Trevor Payne presented the idea for a gospel youth choir to Reverend Frank Gabural and Daisy Seeney. The original choir of forty male and female singers met at the Union United Church. This unique choir performed classical, modern and Black gospel music. The group have made several television appearances and have recorded three albums. The choir has toured Canada and the United States under the direction of Trevor Payne and Sam Batiste.

In 1982, the matured members of the choir were brought together to commemorate the 75th anniversary of Union United Church. `The New Jubilation Gospel Choir was created, and became the first gospel choir to perform at the Stratford Music Festival in 1984. This group has established itself as Canada's leading Gospel Choir, performing at jazz festivals in Montreal, Toronto and Ottawa. The choir recently completed a European tour, establishing gospel music as an international art.

# BURSARIES & AWARDS IN NAMES OF OUTSTANDING BLACKS

Several scholarships have been established for young Black people. The following are just a few of the awards that have been designed to encourage the pursuit of excellence.

## KATHLEEN (KATHY) SEARLES

Kathy Searles was born in Barbados where she was an elementary school teacher. In 1947, she came to Canada to marry her fiance, Edsworth Searles. While raising their own three daughters, Kathy and her husband managed to open their home to early West Indian immigrants, making their lonely days away from their families and friends a little easier.

Their daughter, Sylvia remembers her mother and father working in organizations such as: the Home Service Association, the Toronto United Negro Association, the UNIA, Universal Negro Improvement Association, which later changed its name to UAIA, the Universal African Improvement Association, the BME Church and others. Kathy served on the board of governors of Caribana, the Toronto West Indian Community's tribute to Canada's Centennial.

The Searles, along with other concerned Blacks, pooled their resources to form the Toronto Negro Credit Union which lent down-payments to early Blacks needing money to put down on homes when the banks would not lend to them.

Kathy's name is associated with the founding of Saturday morning remedial classes for Black students beginning in 1969. This was the forerunner of the Black Education Project. Searles worked through the education system, visiting schools, setting up parent-teacher groups.

In 1988, Mrs. Searles received the first Kay Livingstone Award from the Ontario Region of the Black Women's Congress for outstanding community service. In addition, a special Kathy Searles Award to an outstanding Black university student was founded in 1988 by the Barbados St. Michael Alumni in Toronto.

## THE KATHY SEARLES AWARD

A university student, Neil Johnson, was the first student to receive the annual Kathy Searles Award in October, 1988. The York University student was proud to accept the award.

Prior to the award presentation by Searles, Cyrline Taylor, chairperson of the Scholarship Fund Committee, described Searles as a pioneer of many of the school policies that are now taken for granted and an outstanding role model.

## HARRY GAIREY

Harry Gairey received the Order of Ontario and the Order of Canada in 1987 for his many outstanding contributions to the community. In 1973, he received the National Black Coalition Community Award, the Islander Publication's Award in 1976 and the Order of Distinction in 1977 from the Jamaican Government. Along with Dr. Carrie Best, he was honoured for his work on behalf of Caribbean immigrants at an African Heritage Celebration held in Halifax in 1988.

Mr. Gairey was born in Jamaica in 1988, grew up in Cuba and came to Canada just before the first World War. He helped to found the Negro Citizenship Association and was a charter member of the Toronto branch of the Universal Negro Improvement Association. Following his retirement, he and other activists organized the West Indian Federation Club.

Perhaps Gairey is best noted for his assistance to newly-arrived West Indian domestics and his interest and work helping to pave the way for Black immigrants coming to Canada.

Mr. Gairey's book entitled A Black Man's Toronto was edited by Donna Hill and was published by the Multicultural History Society of Ontario in 1981.

## HARRY GAIREY SCHOLARSHIPS

The first Harry Gairey Scholarships of $1000 each were presented at the Old Mill Restaurant in Toronto in 1986. Three students - Carlene Banton, Carla Hall and Paula Tracey were the first recipients.

In 1987, two Toronto high school students each received $1000 to pursue studies at the university level. The scholarships are awarded to students who have achieved the Ontario Secondary School Diploma plus six Ontario academic courses by June of a given academic year and who have registered in a recognized program of higher education. The student must demonstrate either at school, or in the wider community, a commitment to serving others.

## THE HERB CARNEGIE FUTURE ACES SCHOLARSHIP

In May, 1989 the Future Aces Foundation presented its first Herb Carnegie Scholarships. Five students from the North York Board received post-secondary scholarships to help pay their tuition to the college or university of their choice. The winners of the scholarships were John Pelletier, Petra McGann, Debby Manstan, Pamela Vrensen and Rick Chang. They also received Future Aces certificates signed by the school principals and Herb Carnegie.

The outstanding grade 13 candidates of any culture or faith, must be between 17 and 24 years of age. Applicants must include a letter from a member of the educational field as well as one from the community.

Herb Carnegie, who was born in Toronto of West Indian parents. He has had a long sports career in hockey with the Quebec Aces. He has helped pave the way for Blacks in Canadian hockey.

As well as excelling in hockey, Herb has also been one of Canada's leading golfers. In 1977, he won the Canadian Amateur Golf Championship. Herb, who is a financial planner, has been recognized by the Government of Ontario, the city of North York and has received the Queen's Silver Jubilee Medal.

## EVA SMITH SCHOLARSHIP

From the day Eva Smith came to Canada from Jamaica in 1956, she has continued to be a caring and involved person. An activist in the Black community, she has played an important role in the Jamaican Canadian Association for many years. She is a founding member of the Women's Committee in the JCA.

After twenty years of volunteer service, including several years in the Jane and Finch area, Eva received a Volunteer Service Award from the Ministry of Citizenship and Culture. She also served as a member of the Ladies League at the BME Church and the Advisory Council which awards Ontario Citizenship Medals.

Eva is Vice President of Toronto's group of women for PACE, a volunteer organization which promotes advancement of Early Childhood Education throughout Jamaica.

Before coming to Canada on a domestic recruitment program, Eva worked as a dental nurse in Jamaica. She later married Ed Smith in Toronto and raised two daughters while working at I.B.M. and Scarborough General Hospital. She was later employed as Program Co-ordinator at J.C.A. In 1982, she worked with the North York Board of Education as a School Community Outreach Worker with the Vanier Family of Schools.

For sometime, Eva has been involved with heritage programs and she is a firm believer in continuing education for mature people.

She has worked actively with the Social Planning Council with the objective of opening a much-needed Youth Shelter in North York. She continually stresses the necessity of Black youth seeing role models and having a good rapport with them. Eva has become a foremost authority on Black youth. An Eva Smith Bursary was launched in October, 1985 by the Caribbean Canadian Youth Association in Toronto.

## JOHN BROOKS SCHOLARSHIP

In 1981, the John Brooks community Scholarship Fund was set up to encourage and foster the pursuit of excellence among students attending Junior High or Secondary Schools in Ontario.

The John Brooks Award is sponsored by the Canadian Caribbean Excelsior Organization. It has been presented to over 200 outstanding students in the form of plaques, trophies and cash.

The scholarships are open to Ontario students from grade 7 through 13 who excel in academics and maintain a seventy percent average. Special recognition is given to students in music, sports, art, dancing, poetry and public speaking.

John Brooks, a long time community worker from Jamaica, is considered an outstanding role model for young people. He has been involved in raising money for Bellevue Hospital in Jamaica and has served as founder and president of the National Domino League of Canada.

After coming to Toronto over 26 years ago, Brooks continued to be committed to the community. From 1964 to 1974, he co-owned and operated the Latin Quarter, a Caribbean-oriented Night Club which encouraged West Indian immigrants and friends to drop in.

Brooks, an active member of the St.Cads Anglican Church, organized sports activities for the Youth Council Organization with the police and served on the Board of the St. Cads Anglican Day Care for 13 years. In 1975, John helped establish the Regal Road Public School Day Care Project in cooperation with the Toronto Board of Education.

Brooks, who has been awarded the Ontario Medal for Good Citizenship, has helped raise funds for the Friends of Africa Relief; the Ethiopian Famine Relief; Hands Across Jamaica Hospital Fund and the Jamaican Bobsled Team.

## DELOS ROGEST DAVIS MEMORIAL SCHOLARSHIP

Delos Rogest Davis was the first Black person to be called to the bar in Canada. He practised law in Amherstburg and Essex County, Ontario until his retirement in 1909. Davis was actively involved in the Black community and he became a member of the King's Council in 1908.

In May 1985, a $500 Rogest Davis Memorial Scholarship was established for Black students in their third year of studies at the Windsor Law School. The scholarship is awarded on the basis of academic standing and involvement in the Black community. The Scholarship was founded by Jacinth Herbert and a committee of law students at the University of Windsor with the hope that other Ontario Law Schools would set up similar bursaries.

## THE BEVERLEY MARGARET REYNOLDS MEMORIAL SCHOLARSHIP

In 1988 the Beverley Margaret Reynolds Memorial Scholarship of $500 was established in memory of Reynolds who died in 1987 of cancer. The scholarship, funded by a committee called the Friends of the BMR Scholarship, welcomes contributions. A fund-raising function is held in the spring. The scholarship is to recognize an outstanding student in Third World Studies at York University (Atkinson) and is awarded annually to a student doing an outstanding research paper relating to the general area of Third World.

Reynolds was employed at York University from 1973 until her death in 1987. While at York she received a B.A. degree in Sociology in 1985.

She was born in Jamaica in 1948, spend most of her early years in England and came to Canada at the age of twenty.

## THE LEON BYNOE MEMORIAL SCHOLARSHIP

In 1987 Metro Toronto Housing Authority Scholarship was named after Leon Bynoe, a former M.T.H.A. recreation coordinator who died in November, 1986 at the age of 29. Bynoe, originally from St. Vincent, was a top basketball player in high school for the Oakwood Barons and later played for Canada's National team.

The $10,000 scholarship is administered by the University of Toronto, and one thousand a year is awarded to an M.T.H.A. resident applicant who meets the scholastic requirements set out by the University.

The M.T.H.A. staff raised the money through various events and private contributions. Bynoe's mother, Ulcina Bynoe present the University of Toronto with a $4,000 cheque to make up the balance of the scholarship fund.

## JAMAICAN CANADIAN ASSOCIATION ALUMNI SCHOLARSHIPS

The Jamaican Canadian Association Alumni Scholarships are awarded to outstanding students in need of financial assistance. The fund was established in 1987 in celebration of the twenty-fifth anniversary of Jamaican independence.

## LINCOLN ALEXANDER AWARD

The Lincoln Alexander award was created in 1992 in order to recognize the work of individuals trying to improve race relations. The annual award will be presented to an Ontario Grade twelve or thirteen student planning to attend a post-secondary institution. The second award will be presented to a non-student between the ages of sixteen and twenty-five.

## HARRY JEROME AWARD

Harry Jerome was one of Canada's outstanding athletes. He was a bronze medallist in the one hundred metres in the 1964 Tokyo Olympics. He won the gold medal at the Pan American and Commonwealth Games in Jamaica in 1966 and was named the Athlete of the Century in British Columbia. In 1971, Jerome was presented the Order of Canada. He was concerned with the image of amateur sports and tried to develop a more positive attitude among athletes in international competition. Suddenly, in 1982, Harry Jerome suffered from a fatal brain seizure. In 1983, Jerome's friends and family decided to establish the Harry Jerome Commemorative Society in an effort to keep his memory alive and to foster pride in Canada's heroes.

The Harry Jerome Awards have become one of the largest Black events of the year. It is intended to encourage Black youths to strive for excellence in everything they do.

The Black Business and Professionals (BPA) established an annual scholarship fund to provide financial assistance to deserving young people. The $2000 scholarships are awarded to students who demonstrate academic excellence, artistic talent, athletic skills and a commitment to the community.

# FILM AND VIDEO BY BLACK WOMEN

1. ANOTHER LOVE STORY
Debbie Douglas, Gabrielle Micallef
1990, 3/4 inch video, 30'
Ontario.

This video uses an entertaining TV melodrama style interspersed with street interviews and direct-to-camera information to focus on an interracial lesbian couple forced to confront all their comfortable notions about aids.

2. BLACK MOTHER, BLACK DAUGHTER
Claire Prieto, Sylvia Hamilton
1989, 16mm colour, 30'
Nova Scotia

Two generations of Nova Scotian Black women explore the social and historical forces that shaped their lives. Prieto, born in Trinidad, and Hamilton, from Nova Scotia, collaborated on this landmark project to explore the specific dynamics of women's histories in the Black communities of the province. They find understandable conflicts across generation and between urban and rural women, but above all a strong sense of continuity that roots these women in all their foremothers experiences.

4. D-E-S-I-R-E
Glace W. Lawrence
1989, 16mm b/w, 3.5'
Ontario

In a few short minutes, D-E-S-I-R-E gets to the heart of the beauty dilemma for Black women. A woman, clearly Afrocentric, flips through a magazine and finds no images she can call her own. Her reaction is clear, clean and final.

6. EATING RIGHT
Claire Prieto
1981, a slide tape presentation for the
Immigrant Women's Centre, Toronto.

7. FAR FROM HOME
Claire Prieto
1986-87, a slide/tape presentation for
the Immigrant Women's Centre, Toronto.

7. FAR FROM HOME
Claire Prieto
1986-87, a slide/tape presentation for
the Immigrant Women's Health Centre, Toronto.


8. HEADSTART '77
Claire Prieto
1977, a slide/tape presentation for Black Resources
and Information Centre, Toronto.


9. HOME FEELING: STRUGGLE FOR A COMMUNITY
Jennifer Hodge de Silva
1983, 16mm colour, 60'
Ontario

A landmark film in Black Canadian cinema, this powerful documentary explores the difficult relations between police and the Black community in a Toronto public housing neighbourhood. Hodge de Silva's methods are subtle, but there's a fire in every frame of this film that has given it a lasting power. Simply by allowing the community and the police to speak for themselves, she encourages the police to convict themselves, and the strength of the community's conviction to shine through.

10. HOME TO BUXTON
Claire Prieto
1987, 16mm colour, 30'
Ontario

Recovering a history unknown to most Canadians, Prieto's film looks at past and present life in the southern Ontario community of North Buxton, last stop on the Underground Railway. This is one of the best-loved films about rural black communities in Canada, lavishing an extraordinary care on the details of life in Buxton, and the history of the people who settled there.


11. JODIE DRAKE; BLUES IN MY BREAD
Christene Browne
1991, 3/4" video, 30'
Ontario

Blues and Jazz singer Jodie Drake is a legend. From her beginnings in Detroit to her many years breaking ground in Canada, she has consistently promoted Black music, often simply through the power of her voice. Blues in My Bread, made for a CBC national broadcast, presents the woman in all her glory. Browne had full access to the singer, her interviews and performances combined with now rare footage from Drake's TV appearances in the 60s and 70s adds an important chapter to the history of jazz and blues music in Canada.

12. MAIGRE DOG
Donna James
1990, 3/4" col. video, 5'
Nova Scotia

James short tape is a remarkable evocation of the subtle power of common knowledge. Using phrases, expressions and homilies she heard over and over again growing up in a West Indian family, James gives the significance and respect. The setting is a kitchen and the voices familiar. But out of this seemingly mundane material, James makes quiet magic.

13. NO CHOICE
Christene Browne
1990, 16mm colour, 8'
Ontario

Made for the National Film Board anthology series, Five Feminist Minutes, No Choice examines the impact of the abortion debate on young women living in poverty. Browne's audacious thesis is that for poor women, abortion is not a simple matter of adopting a 'pro-choice' or 'pro-life' position. For these women, abortion is an issue controlled by the same social institutions that regulate their poverty. For these women, it's often impossible to be pro-choice when there is no choice.

14. OLDER, STRONGER, WISER
Claire Prieto, Dionne Brand
1990, 16mm colour, 30'
Ontario

A portrait of older Black women in Ontario-rural and urban-whose lives are testaments to overcoming adversity. Directed by pioneer Black filmmaker Claire Prieto, this film speaks from an urgent need to recover obscured or untold histories. These women's struggles against racial and sexual injustices span decades. Their lives are lessons for us all.

15. SISTERS IN THE STRUGGLE
Directors: Dionne Brand, Ginny Stikeman
Producer: Ginny Stikeman

Sisters in the Struggle is a film about contemporary Black women activists, of varying ages and backgrounds, involved in the movements against racism and sexism in Canada. The activists are women in the labour movement, in community organizing, in electoral politics, in anti-poverty organizing and in feminist organizing. Their analysis links these struggles with the ongoing battle against pervasive racism and systemic violence against women and people of colour that exists in Canada.

16. SOME BLACK WOMEN
Claire Prieto
1976-77, 16mm documentary,
Toronto.


17. THE CHALLENGE OF DIVERSITY
Claire Prieto
1989, video produced by CBC and others
Toronto.


18. THIS ALIENATION
Nicole Thompson
1992, 3/4" col. video, 12'
British Columbia

Thompson's carefully observed tape expresses the feelings of just about every Black immigrant who came from a warm climate to a Canadian winter. Sitting on her bed casually reminiscing, she takes us through all the poses, denials, pleasures and discomforts with which we all greet the cold and ice.

19. TRACES
Julia Browne Figuereo
1991, 16mm col., 4'
Quebec

A fresh, fast-paced jet tour of African roots. On a trip to the continent, a young woman discovers just how much African women have in common with their Caribbean and Canadian counterparts.


20. UNNATURAL CAUSES
Lillian Allen
1990, 16mm film-poem, 7 min.
National Film Board, Studio D

A fast-paced montage that challenges the official post-card-perfect image of Canadian society. The film is based on Allen's highly acclaimed Album Conditions Critical.


21. WOMEN AND WORK IN THE THIRD WORLD
Claire Prieto
1986, Emma Productions
Toronto.

## SOME BOOKS BY SISTER VISION PRESS: BLACK WOMEN AND WOMEN OF COLOUR

ADISA, OPAL PALMER
 Tamarind and Mango Women, 'a Collection of Poetry'.
 (Sister Vision Press, Toronto, Ontario 1992)
 ISBN 0-920813-71-2

BASKIN, CINDY
 The Invitation
 (Sister Vision Press, Toronto, Ontario 1992)
 ISBN 0-920813-54-2

BANNERJI, HIMANI
 Coloured Pictures, 'a Book for Young People.'
 - Illustrator- SASSO. (Sister Vision Press,
 Toronto, Ontario 1991)
 ISBN 0-920813-86-0

 Doing Time
 (Sister Vision Press, 1991) ISBN 0-920813-01-1

 Re: Turing the Gaze
 - Essays on Racism, Feminism and Politics
 (Sister Vision Press, 1993) ISBN 0-920813-55-0

BRAITHWAITE, RELLA and TESSA BENN-IRELAND
 Some Black Women.
 (Sister Vision Press, Toronto, Ontario 1992)
 ISBN 0-920813-84-4

BRAITHWAITE, DIANA
 Martha and Elvira
 (Sister Vision Press, 1993)
 ISBN 0-920813-64-X

BRAND, DIONNE
 Earth Magic, Children Poems.
 (Sister Vision Press, 1993)

COOPER, AFUA
 The Red Caterpillar on College Street.
 (Sister Vision Press, Toronto, Ontario 1989)
 ISBN 0-920813-87-9

 Memories Have Tongue.
 (Sister Vision Press, Toronto, Ontario 1992)
 ISBN 0-920813-50-X

DEHAARTE, NORMA
    Guyana Betrayal
    (Sister Vision Press, Toronto, Ontario 1991)
    ISBN 0-920813-80-1

ESCAMILLA, KLEYA FORTE
    Mada
    (Sister Vision Press, 1993)
    ISBN 0-920813-69-0

ESPINET, RAMABAI,
    Nuclear Season
    (Sister Vision Press, 1991)
    ISBN 0-920813-61-5

    The Princess of Spadina- a Tale of Toronto
    - a Children's Book
    - Illustrator, VERONICA SULLIVAN
    (Sister Vision Press, 1992)
    ISBN 0-920813-66-6

ESPINET, RAMABAI (editor)
    Creation Fire- Anthology of Caribbean Women Writers
    (Sister Vision Press, Toronto, Ontario 1990)
    ISBN 0-920813-02-X

FIFE, CONNIE
    Beneath the Naked Sun
    (Sister Vision Press, Toronto, Ontario 1992)
    ISBN 0-920813-59-3

    The Colour of Resistance
    - Collection of Works by First Nations Women
    (Sister Vision Press, Toronto, Ontario 1992)
    ISBN 0-920813-62-3

FRENCH, JOAN
    Wid Dis Ring
    (Sister Vision Press, Toronto, Ontario 1987)
    ISBN 0-920813-83-6

HANIFF, Z NESHA
    Blaze A Fir
    (Sister Vision Press, 1991) ISBN 0-920813-91-7

HENDERSON, PETA, and BRYN HOUGHTON
    Rise Up: Life Stories of Belizean Women
    - By the Women of the Orange Walk District
    (Sister Vision Press, Toronto, Ontario 1993)
    ISBN 0-920813-78-X

MAGUIRE, DIANNE
　　Dry Land Tourist-A Collection of Short Stories
　　(Sister Vision Press, Toronto, Ontario 1991)
　　ISBN 0-920813-67-4

MANDIELA, AHDRI ZHINA
　　Speshal Rikwes
　　(Sister Vision Press, Toronto, Ontario 1985)

　　Dark Diaspora.
　　(Sister Vision Press, Toronto, Ontario 1992)

MONTAGUE, CHARMAINE
　　Dread Culture
　　(Sister Vision Press, Toronto, Ontario 1993)
　　ISBN 09208 13-53-4

SEARS, DJANET
　　Africa Solo
　　(Sister Vision Press, Toronto, Ontario 1990)
　　ISBN 0-920813-00-3

SILVERA, MAKEDA
　　Silenced
　　(Sister Vision Press, Toronto. Second Edition 1989)
　　(first edition published by Williams-Wallace in 1983)

　　Remembering G and Other Stories
　　(Sister Vision Press, Toronto, Ontario 1991)
　　ISBN 0-920813-60-7

　　Piece of My Heart: A Lesbian of Colour Anthology.
　　(Sister Vision Press, Toronto, Ontario 1991)
　　ISBN 0-920813-65-8

　　Growing Up Black- A Manual For Black Youths
　　(Sister Vision Press, Toronto, Ontario, 1989)

SISTREN WITH HONOR FORD-SMITH
　　Lionheart Gal
　　(Sister Vision Press, Toronto, Ontario 1987)
　　ISBN 0-920813-90-9

SRIVASTAVA, VINITA
　　A Giant Named Azalea
　　(Sister Vision Press, 1991)
　　ISBN 0-920813-68-2

TAMAI, KOBAYASHI and MONA OIKAWA
　All Names Spoken
　(Sister Vision Press, Toronto,Ontario 1992)
　ISBN 0-920813-88-7

ROY, LYNETTE
　Brown Girl in the Ring, a Biography for Young People.
　(Sister Vision Press, 1992)
　ISBN 0-9 20813-52-6

KEESHIG-TOBIAS, LENORE
　Running on the March Wind
　- Other Dreams and References
　(Sister Vision Press, Toronto, Ontario 1992)
　ISBN 0-920813-48-8

　Bird Talk Bineshiinh Dibaajmowin
　(illustrator-POLLY KEESHIG-TOBIAS
　(Sister Vision Press, Toronto, Ontario 1992)
　ISBN 0-920813-89-5

TROTMAN, ALTHEA
　How the East Pond Got It's Flowers
　(Sister Vision Press, 1991
　ISBN 0-920813-85-2

　How the Star Fish Got to the Sea
　(Sister Vision Press, 1992)
　ISBN 0-9208-13-70-4

　Ladies of the Night: Short Stories
　(Sister Vision Press,1993)

WORDS ARE WHAT I'VE GOT
　Complied by the International Task Force on Literacy-
　Writings by Learners from all around the World
　during International Literacy Year
　(Sister Vision Press, 1991)
　ISBN 0-920813-46-1

MANAGING EDITORS- MAKEDA SILVERA AND NILA GUPTA
　Women of Colour Speak Out: The Issue is 'ism
　(Sister Vision Press, Toronto, Ontario 1983)
　ISBN 0-920813-72-0

# SOME BOOKS BY BLACK CANADIAN WOMEN

ALLEN, CAROL and ELWIN, ROSAMUND
　Getting Wet: Tales of Lesbian Seduction
　(Women's Press, 1992)

ALLEN, CAROL
　'The Report Card.' Dykeversion: Lesbian Short Fiction.
　(Women's Press, 1986)

ALLEN, LILLIAN
　Rythm an' Hardtimes. (Well Versed, 1992)
　Nothing But a Hero. (Well Versed)
　Why Me? (Well Versed, 1991)

BLACK, AYANNA
　No Contingencies. (Williams-Wallace Publishers, Toronto, 1986)

BRAMBLE, LINDA
　Black Fugitive Slaves in Early Canada. (Vanwell Publishing
　Company, St. Catherines, Ontario, 1988)

BRAND, DIONNE
　Chronicles of the Hostile Sun
　(Williams-Wallce, Toronto, 1984)

　Winter Epigrams and Epigrams to Ernesto Cardenal
　in Defense of Claudia
　(Williams-Wallace, Toronto, 1983)

　Primitive Offense
　(Williams-Wallace International Inc., Toronto, 1982)

　Fore Day Morning
　(Khosian Artists, Toronto, 1978)

　No Language is Neutral
　(Coach House Press, 1990)

　Sans Souci and Other Stories
　(Williams-Wallace Publishers, Toronto, 1988)

　No Burden to Carry
　(Narratives of Black working families inOntario.
　1920's to 1950's)
　Women's Press, 1991.

CREIDER, JANE TAPSUBEI
  The Shrunken Dream
  (Women's PRess, 1992)

CROMWELL, LIZ
  One Out of Many - A Collection of Writings by Black
  Women in Ontario
  (A WACRACO Production, Toronto, 1975)

D'OYLEY, ENID
  Between Sea and Sky
  (Williams-Wallace International,1979)

  Animals Fables and other Tales Retold
  (Williams-Wallace International, 1982)

  The Bridge of Dreams
  (Williams-Wallace, 1984)

EDER, DOROTHY
  The Computer Centre Party: Canada Meets Black
  Power. (Tundra Books, Montreal, 1969)

ELWIN, ROSAMUND and PAULSE, MICHELE
  'The Moonlight — Hide-and-Seek Club'
  in The Pollution Solution
  (Women's Press, 1992)

  Asha's Mums
  (Women's Press, 1988)

FRASER, J.C.
  Cry of the Illegal Immigrant
  (Williams-Wallace International,1980)

HARRIS, CLAIRE
    Drawing Down a Daughter
    (Goose Lane Press, 1992)

    Fable From the Women's Quarters
    (Williams-Wallace, Toronto)

    The Conception of Winter
    (Williams-Wallace, Toronto)

    19 Travelling to Find a Remedy
    (Goose Lane Editions, Toronto)
    ISBN 0-88795-022-1

    Translation into Fiction
    (Fiddlehead Poetry Book and Goose Lane Editions Ltd.)

KALLEN, EVELYN
    Anatomy of Racism in Canadian Dimension
    (Harvest House, Montreal, 1974)

LEWIS, THERESA
    'They Put 'im So.'
    Other Voices, edited by Lorris Elliot
    (Williams-Wallace Publishers)

PHILIP, NOURBESE, MARLENE
    Poetry Thorns
    (Salmon Courage- Williams-Wallace)

    She Tries Her Tongue, Her Silence Softly Breaks
    (Ragweed Publishers)

    Harriet's Daughter
    (Women's Press, 1988)

PERRY, CHARLOTTE
    The Long Road: History of the Coloured Canadian in
    Windsor, Ontario, 1867-1967
    (Summer Press, Windsor, Ontario)

SILVERA, MAKEDA
Fireworks: The Best of Fireweed
(Women's Press, 1986)

TALBOT, CAROL
Growing Up Black in Canada
(Williams-Wallace Publishers Inc. Toronto, 1984)

THORNVALDSON, PATRICIA
Identity: The Black Experience in Canada
Ontario Education
Comm. Authority and Gage Publishers 1979

TYNES, MAXINE
Woman Talking Woman
(Pottersfield Press, 1990)

Borrowed Beauty
(Pottersfield Press, Nova Scotia, 1987)

WILLIAMS, DOROTHY
Blacks in Montreal, 1628-1986: An Urban Demography
(Edition Yvon Blais Inc., Cowansville, Quebec, 1989)

VAN DYKE, JANICE BANIGAN
Like the Leaves. (Summer Printing and Publishing Co. Ltd., Windsor, 1972)

## QUICK FACTS ON BLACKS

### 1608-1990

1608     Mattheiu da Costa, a slave, is the first known black to land in Canada at Port Royal, now Annapolis Royal, Nova Scotia. In Hill, Daniel G. 'The Freedom Seekers' blacks in early Canada. Agincourt, Book Society of Canada Ltd., 1981.

1628     Olive le Jeune, a boy from Madagascar was the first recorded slave purchase in New France. In Black Studies; a resource guide for teachers. Ontario. Ministry of Education, 1983.

1685     The "code noir" became law in France. "Code Noir" or Black Code provided guidance on issues such as sale of slaves, religious instruction, training and disposition of offspring. In Black Studies; a resource guide for teachers. Ontario. Ministry of Education. 1983.

1709     Slavery became legal in France. In Black Studies; a resource guide for teachers. Ontario. Ministry of Education. 1983.

1734     Marie Joseph Angelique, a slave girl set fire to her mistress house in an attempted escape. She was later captured and hung. In Black Studies; a resource guide for teachers. Ontario Ministry of Education. 1983.

1777     Slaves in Canada escaped to Vermont where slavery had been abolished. In Black Studies; a resource guide for teachers. Ontario Ministry of Education. 1983.

1783     Black Loyalists from the United States established communities in Nova Scotia. In Grant, John N., Black Nova Scotians. Halifax, N.S. Nova Scotia Museum.

1784 Former white soldiers, unemployed or unwilling to work at the wages paid to free blacks, rampage in Birchtown and Shelburne, Nova Scotia; troops are called in to restore order. In Hill, Daniel G. The Freedom Seekers. Agincourt. The Book Society of Canada Ltd. 1981.

1785 A black loyalist, John Marrant, returned from England to Nova Scotia and established a Huntingdonian congregation among the Black population of Birchtown. In Blacks Studies; a resource guide for teachers. Ontario Ministry of Education. 1983.

1792 A fleet consisting of 1,190 persons, 222 of them from New Brunswick left Halifax Harbour bound for Africa. On board were groups from Shelbourne, Digby, Preston, Halifax, Saint John and other black communities. In Grant, John N., Black Nova Scotians..1980.

1792 Black Loyalists in Nova Scotia and New Brunswick migrated to Sierra Leone, West Africa because promises of free land and full equity had not been fulfilled in Canada. In Black Studies; a resource guide for teachers...1983.

1792 Josiah (Joseph) Cutten, convicted for stealing some rum and furs, is the first person officially executed in Upper Canada. In Hill, Daniel G. The Freedom Seekers, 1981.

1793 Upper Canada prohibits the "further introduction of slaves", but did not free those already in slavery. In Hill, Daniel G. The Freedom Seekers...1981.

1796 June 26, three transports, the Dover, Mary and Anne sailed from Port Royal Harbour Jamaica. 543 Maroon men, women and children arrived in Halifax approx. one month later. In Grant, John N. Black Nova Scotians...1980.

1807     Simon Fitch of Wolfiville purchased a woman named Nelly, for 93 (pound) it was considered the last slave sale in Nova Scotia. In Grant, John N. Black Nova Scotians...1980.

1813     A company of Niagara Blacks goes on alert to defend Ontario against a United States invasion. In Thompson, Colin A. Blacks in Deep Snow. Don Mills, Ont. Dent and Sons. 1979.

1814     Richard Preston arrived in Halifax seeking his mother who had preceded him north. Determined to find her he sought shelter at a house along the way. The door was opened by his mother who recognized her long lost son by a scar on his face. In Grant, John N. Nova Scotians....1980.

1817     A census of the Black Community at Tracadie showed several persons to be of Jamaican ancestry. In Grant, John N. Black Nova Scotians...1980.

1821     The First Baptist Church is established in Colchester County, Nova Scotia, with Elder Wilkes as Pastor. In Grant, John, N. Black Nova Scotians....1980.

1822     Black settlers in Tracadie, Nova Scotia established the Tracadie United Church, Canada's oldest United Church. In Shreve, Dorothy Shadd., The Afro Canadian Church: a stabilizer Jordan Station...1983.

1828     The Coloured Wesleyan Methodist Church Founded. In Shreve, Dorothy Shadd., The Afro Canadian Church: a stabilizer Jordan Station...1983.

1829   The Executive Council of Lower Canada refuses to extradite refuge slave Paul Vallard to the United States....In Hill, Daniel G. The Freedom Seekers. 1981.

1830   Josiah Henson, said to be inspirational for Uncle Tom's cabin, escapes with his wife and children to freedom in what was then known as Canada West. In Bramble, Linda. Black Fugitive Slaves in early Canada. St. Catharines, Ontario, Vanwell Publishing Ltd. 1968.

1832   Richard Preston organized the African baptist Church on Cornwallis Street in Halifax, Nova Scotia. In Grant, John N. Nova Scotians....1980.

1834   An act of the British Parliament abolishes slavery throughout the colonies, freeing nearly 800.000 slaves. In Thompson, Colin A. Blacks in Deep Snow; Black pioneers in Canada. Don Mills, Ontario, Dent & Sons. 1979.

1837   The anti-slavery society of Canada organizes to press for abolition across the continent. In Pemberton, Ian C. The anti-slavery society of Canada. Toronto.
University of Toronto. M.A. Thesis., 1967.

1840   Ellen Toyer Abbott founds the Queen Victorian Benevolent Society. In Hill, Daniel G. The Freedom Seekers..1981.

1841   Beginning of Dawn Settlement in Canada West, now know as Dresden, Ontario.
In Black Studies; a resource guide for teachers, Ontario Ministry of Education. 1983.

| | |
|---|---|
| 1842 | Fifteen schools established in Amherstburg, Toronto and Oro by Canada mission. In Black Studies; a resource guide for teachers. Ontario Ministry of Education. 1983. |
| 1843 | Henry Gray chaired a committee of 20 Blacks to organize the Emancipation Day Celebrations. In Hill, Daniel G. The Freedom Seekers. 1981. |
| 1845 | Amherstburg Regular Missionary Baptist Association established itself after disputes with white Baptist groups in Michigan and Western Canada. In Hill, Daniel G. The Freedom Seekers...1981. |
| 1846 | Dr. William Harvey Goler, a Black Nova Scotian becomes the first Black President of a college. In Grant, John N. Black Nova Scotians...1980. |
| 1851 | Harriet Tubman began her journeys, ferrying slaves across the border on the Underground Railroad. She made 19 trips guiding slaves to freedom in North America. In Black Studies: a resource guide for teachers...1983. |
| 1851 | Formation of the Toronto Anti-Slavery society. In Hubbard C. Against All Odds. |
| 1851-52 | Uncle Tom's Cabin, by Harriet Beecher Stowe, is published in Toronto and Montreal. Ontario Black History Society Records. |
| 1852 | Henry Bibb published and distributed the anti-slavery harp, a collection of popular anti-slavery songs. In Hill, Daniel G. The Freedom Seekers. 1981. |

1853    Mary Ann Shadd and Family launch the Provincial Freeman in Windsor, Ontario. It was
        published sporadically until 1859. In Black Studies: a resource guide for teachers...1983.

1854    Richard Preston, at Granville Mountain met with delegates of twelve African Baptist
        churches to form the African Baptist Association of Nova Scotia.
        In Grant, John N. Black Nova Scotians...1980.

1854    The True Band, a benevolent society for men and women was formed in Malden, and spread
        across Canada West. It encouraged refugees to take an interest in one another's welfare, to
        cooperate in economic ventures, to improve their schools and unite their churches.
        In Hill, Daniel G. The Freedom Seekers. 1981.

1854    The Provincial Union Association was formed. It proposed a broad program for the refugees
        of Canada West. In Hill, Daniel G. The Freedom Seekers. 1981.

1854    The Formation of the African Baptist Association of Nova Scotia. In Black Studies; a guide
        for teachers Ontario Ministry of Education. 1983.

1855    Emaline Shadd receives top honours, first prize, and a first class teaching certificate from
        the Normal School in Toronto. In Hill, Daniel G. The Freedom Seekers...1981.

1856    Formation of the British Methodist Episcopal Church (B.M.E.) Rev. Willis Nazrey became the
        first bishop of the B.M.E. church. In Walker, James W. St. G., A History of Blacks in Canada;
        a study guide for teachers and students. Ontario Ministry of State Multiculturalism...1980.

1857    T.F. Carey and R.B. Richards, start Toronto's first ice company, drawing their stock from Mill Ponds around Bloor Street. In Hill, Daniel G. The Freedom Seekers. 1981.

1857    William Edward Hall, the son of a slave from Virginia is the first Canadian to be awarded the Victorian Cross –- the most highly prized of all English Military medals. A Branch of the Royal Legion in Halifax bears his name. In Ruck, Calvin W. The Black Battalion; 1916-1920. Canada's best kept secret. Halifax, Nova Scotia. Nimbus Published. 1987.

1859    John Brown and his abolitionist companions attack Harper's Ferry, West Virginia. The year before, Brown had visited Chatham, Ontario, where he stayed at the home of Black poet James Madison Bell. In Ebony Pictorial History of America. Vol.I. 1971. Chicago, Johnson Publ.

1859    Abraham Shadd became the first Canadian black elected to public office.
In Black Studies; a resource guide for teachers. Ontario Ministry of Education. 1983.

1860    The all Black Victorian Riffle Corps was formed to defend British Columbia.
In Black Studies; a resource guide for teachers, Ontario Ministry of Education...1983.

1861    Dr. Anderson Ruffin Abbott became the first Canadian born black to graduate from the University of Toronto Medical School. He later served as coroner of Kent County and Chief Resident Physician of Toronto General Hospital.
In Black Studies; a resource guide for teachers, Ontario Ministry of Education...1983.

1863    The Emancipation Proclamation was passed in the United States.
In Black Studies; a resource guide for teachers. Ontario Ministry of Education..1983.

| | |
|---|---|
| 1870 | Known as "Little Chocolate" to fight faciers, George Dixon was born in Halifax on July 29. He was the first black Canadian boxer to win 3 world titles; paperweight, bantamweight and featherweight championships at different times. He died in 1909.<br>In Grant, John N. Black Nova Scotians...1980 |
| 1880 | Mary Ann Shadd Cary organizes the Coloured Women's Progressive Association, to fight for women's suffrage and equal rights for women. In Hill, Daniel G. The Freedom Seekers. 1981. |
| 1882 | John Ware, the coloured cowboy, rancher and cow hand in the West introduced longhorn cattle into Canada and pioneered the development of the rodeo. In McEwan, Grant, John Ware Cow Country. Saskatoon, Saskatchewan. Western Producer Prairie Books., 1973. |
| 1885 | Delos Rogest Davis the first black lawyer, is admitted to the Law Society of Upper Canada and goes on to become a King's Counsel in 1910. |
| 1890 | Elijah McCoy, a black Canadian had more than 50 patents for his inventions. His inventions became so popular that people today use the expression "the real McCoy", whenever they speak of something that is genuine or original. In Adams, Russell Great Negroes, Past and Present. Chicago, Ill., African American Publishing. Co. 1972. |
| 1894 | William Peyton Hubbard, Canada's first major Black politician begins public service, first as Toronto's Ward 4 Alderman, and later as the Vice-Chairman of the Board of Control and Acting Mayor of the City of Toronto.<br>In Hubbard, Stephen L. Against all Odds. Toronto, Dundurn Press Ltd. 1987. |

1896     James Robinson Johnson the first black Nova Scotian to graduate from Dalhousie University with a law degree.

1900     Alfred Shadd becomes the first Black Doctor in Melfort, Saskatchewan.
He also ran a farm and became the first president of the melfort Agricultural Society.
In Hill, Daniel G. The Freedom Seekers 1981.

1901     Mary Matilda Winslow became the first black woman to enter the university of New Brunswick. She graduated with honours, winning the Montogomery-Campbell Prize in 1905.
In Women of our Times edited by Enid F. D'Oyley and Rella Braithwaite 1973.

1904     Charles Drew a Black Doctor who attended McGill University, invents a process for storing blood plasma. In Adams, Russell L. Great Negroes, Past and Present. Chicago. Ill., African American Publishing Company 1972.

1909     Matthew A. Henson first black polar explorer who discovered the North Pole. In Ferris, Jeri Arctic Explorer; the story of Matthew Henson. Minneapolis Minn., Carolrhoda Books Inc. 1989.

1911     Portia White world famous contralto born in Truro, Nova Scotia. In Encyclopedia of Music in Canada., University of Toronto Press 1981.

1914     Universal Negro Improvement and Conservation Association and African Communities Leagues launched. In Van Sertima, Ivan ed. Great Black Leaders; ancient and modern. New Brunswick, New Jersey. Journal of African Civilization Ltd. 1988.

1916    Dr. William A. White went overseas with the second construction Batalion as the only black Chaplain in the British Empire. Dr. White was also the first Black Minister to preach at the Baptist convention in Wolfvile. In Grant.. Black Nova Scotians.

1916    Nova Scotia's No.2 Construction Battalion was formed as a segregated unit to enlist blacks for service in the First World War. In Ruck, Calvin W. "The Black Battalion; 1916-1920. Canada's best kept military secret..Halifax, Nova Scotia Nimbus Publishing 1987.

1919    Women's Charitable Benevolent Association formed to look after the poor and sick, to run soup kitchens and to provide temporary homes for returning soldiers.
In Women of our Times..edited by Enid F. D'Oyley and Rella Braithwaite 1973.

1921    Marcus Garvey, a Jamaican began a world movement that fostered the development of Black pride and the appreciation of African heritage. In Canada it led to the formation of chapters of the Universal Negro Improvement Association.
In Black Studies; a resource guide for teachers, Ontario Ministry of Education 1983.

1922    Home Service Association established in Toronto. In Gairey, Harry. A Black Man's Toronto; 1914-1980. Toronto; Multicultural History of Ontario. 1981.

1922    The Phylliss Wheatley Art Club formed by Lillian Rutherford offered cultural development and later developed in the 1930's into the Negro Theatre Guild of Montreal.
In Women of our Times...edited by Enid F. D'Oyley and Rella Braithwaite 1973.

SOME BLACK WOMEN

1944     Ontario passes an Act to prevent the publication of discrimination of matter referring to race or creed. In Statutes of Ontario; 1944. Chapter 51. Toronto, Queen's Printer Publication.

1944     Bernice Redmon trained at St. Phillip Hospital, Medical College of Virginia became the first Canadian born registered nurse to be employed in Public Health in Ontario. In Women of our Times...edited by Enid F. D'Oyley and Rella Braithwaite 1973.

1947     Jackie Robinson became the first black signed to play with the Brooklyn Dodgers major league baseball. In Alder, David A. "Jackie Robinson" he was the first. New York, Holiday Press. 1989.

1948     Ruth Bailey and Gwennyth Barton are the first blacks known to graduate from a Canadian school of Nursing. Ruth Bailey also wins first prize for proficiency. In Women of our Times...edited by Enid F. D'Oyley and Rella Braithwaite 1973.

1951     Addie Aylestock is ordained as a minister of the British Methodist Espicopal Church. In Shreve, Dorothy Shadd. The African Canadian Church a stabilizer. Jordan Station, Ontario, Paideia Press, 1983.

1953     The Canadian Negro, a national newspaper established. In Black Studies; a resource guide for teachers, Ontario Ministry of Education. 1983.

1954     Delegation of Black Canadians met with members of Federal Cabinet to discuss discrimination against West Indians applying to enter Canada. In Black Studies; a resource guide for teachers; An Intermediate Division. Ontario Ministry of Education. 1983.

| | |
|---|---|
| 1955 | The Brotherhood of Sleeping Car Porters won Blacks the right to be promoted to Conductor. In Black Studies; a resource guide for teachers; Intermediate Division. Ontario Ministry of Education 1983. |
| 1958 | Willie O'Rea of New Brunswick becomes the first Black to play hockey in the National Hockey League. In National Hockey League Official Guide Book. |
| 1959 | Stanley G. Grizzle is the first black man to run for the Ontario Legislature in Canada. |
| 1960 | Myrtle Blackwood Smith, the first black women to be called to the Ontario Bar. In Black Studies; a resource guide for teachers; Intermediate Division. Ontario Ministry of Education 1983. |
| 1961 | Calvin Best a black Nova Scotian, was named president of the Civil Service Association. In Black Studies; a resource guide for teachers; Intermediate Division. Ontario Ministry of Education 1983. |
| 1962 | Dr. Daniel Hill appointed Director of Human Rights Commission. In Black Studies; a resource guide for teachers; intermediate Division. Ontario Ministry of Education 1983. |
| 1963 | Leonard Braithwaite is the first black elected to the Ontario Legislature. In Black Studies; a resource guide for teachers; Intermediate Division. Ontario Ministry of Education 1983. |
| 1965 | Malcolm X was killed by assassins in New York City. In Hudson, Wade. Book of Black Heroes; from A to Z. Orange, New Jersey. Just Us Books 1988. |

1967     Caribana Toronto's first caribbean style carnival is organized to commemorate Canada's centennial.

1968     Dr. Martin Luther King. Jr. was assassinated in Memphis Tennessee.
In Hudson, Wade. Book of Black Heroes; from A to Z. Orange, New Jersey. Just Us Books 1988.

1968     Lincoln McCauley Alexander becomes Canada's first black member of Parliament.
In Canadian Parliamentary Guide 1992.

1968     Harry Jerome retires from competitive athletics. He represented Canada in seven international games and was the first man to hold 100 yards and 100 metres record simultaneously.

1969     The National Black Coalition of Canada is born. In Thompson, Colin A., Blacks in Deep Snow; Black pioneers in Canada. Don Mills. J.M. Dent & Sons 1976.

1978     Stanley G. Grizzle first black man appointed Citizenship court Judge in Canada.

1978     The Ontario Black History Society forms with Dr. Daniel G. Hill as the first president and founder.
In Hill, Daniel G. Freedom Seekers 1981.

1983     Guion Bluford, Jr. become American's first black astronaut. In Kallen, Stuart. The Struggle into the 1990's. A history of black people from 1968 to the present. Edina, Minn. Abdo & Daughters 1990.

1984     Anne Clare Cools becomes the first black women appointed to the Senate of Canada.
In Benn-Ireland, Tessa. Black Business and Professional Women's Engagement Calender. Scarborough, Ont. Resources Unlimted 1987.

| | |
|---|---|
| 1984 | Jesse Jackson becomes the first black man to run for President of the United States of America. In Hudson, Wade. Book of Black Heroes; from A to Z. Orange N.J., Just Us Books 1988. |
| 1984 | Mae Ruth Sarsfield becomes the first black woman to serve on the Board of Directors of the Canadian Broadcasting Corporation. |
| 1984 | J. Calbert Best is the first black Canadian to be appointed as an Ambassador. In Black Studies; a resource guide for teachers. Ontario Ministry of Education 1983. |
| 1985 | Lincoln MacCaulay Alexander becomes the first black Lieutenant Governor of Ontario. In Canadian Parliamentary Guide 1992. |
| 1986 | Dr. Ronald E. McNair died in the Challenger explosion. In Lewis, Richard S. Challenger - the final voyage. New York. Columbia University Press 1988. |
| 1987 | Pamela Appelt is the first black woman appointed Citizenship court Judge in Canada. |
| 1989 | Dr. Glenda Simms is the first black women appointed President of the Seventeen year old Canadian Advisory Council on the Status of Women. |
| 1990 | Nelson Mandela was released after spending 10,000 days (27 years) in prison. |
| 1992 | Judge Michelle A. Rawlins becomes the first black woman to be appointed to an Ontario Court bench. |

# BIBLIOGRAPHY

## QUICK FACTS ON BLACKS 1609-1992

Adams, Russel L.
   Great Negroes; Past and Present Chicago III;
   African American Publishing Co. Inc. 1963

Adler, David A.
   Jackie Robinson; he was the first.
   A first biography. New York., Holiday House. 1989

Benn-Ireland, Tessa J.
   The Black Business and Professional Woman's
   Engagement Calendar
   Scarborough, Ont., Resouces Unlimted. 1987

Black Resources; a resource guide for teachers:
   Intermediate Division.
   Ontario Ministry of Education 1983

Bramble, Linda
   Black Business and Professional Woman's
   Engagement Calendar.
   Scarborough, Ont., Resources Unlimted 1987

Canadian Parliamentary Guide
   edited by Kathryn M. Flanagan and Miller, K. J.,
   Toronto. Globe and Mail Pub 1982

Clairmont, Donald H. and Magill, Dennis W.
   Africville: The Life and Death of a Canadian
   Black Community.
   Toronto, Canada Scholar's Press.

D'Oyley, Enid F. and Braithwaite, R.
   Women of our Times. Toronto,
   The Canadian Negro Women's Association Inc. 1973

Ferris, Jeri
   Arctic explorer: The Story of Matthew Henson.
   Minneapolis, Minn. Carolrhoda Books

Grant, John N. N
   Black Nova Scotians  Halifax, N.S.
   Nova Scotia Museum 1980

Hill, Daniel G.
   The Freedom Seekers; Blacks in early Canada.
   Agincourt, Ont., Book Society of Canada 1981

Hubbard, Stephen
   Against all Odds: The Story of William Peyton Hubbard,
   Black leader and municipal reformer.
   Toronto, Dundurn Press, 1987

Hudson, Wade
   Book of Black heroes: From A to Z. Orange, N.J.,
   Just Us Books 1988

Kallen, Stuart
   The Struggle into the 1990's: A History of Black
   people from 1968 to the present.
    Edina, Minn., Abdo & Daughters 1990

Krass, Peter
   Sojourner Truth.
   New York, Chelsea House 1988

Lewis, Richard S.
   Challenger - the final voyage.
   New York., Columbia University Press 1988

MacEwan, Grant
   John Ware's Cow Country
   Saskatoon: Western Producer Prairie Books

McKissack, Patricia and Frederick McKissack
   Frederick Douglas: The Black Lion
   Chicago: Children's Press

Metcalf, Doris Hunter
   Portraits in Black. Carthage, Ill.
   Good Apple Inc. 1990.

National Hockey League Sourcebook
   Toronto. Fitzhenry & Whiteside 1989

Felz, Ruth
   Black Heroes of the Wild West.
   Seattle, Washington Open Hand Publ. Inc. 1990

Quarles, Benjamin
   Black Abolitionists
   New York Da Capo Press 1991

Riendeau, Roger
   An Enduring Heritage: Black contributions to early
   Ontario. (Ministry of Citizenship and Culture)
   Dundurn Press 1984

Ruck, Calvin W.
   The Black Battalion: 1916-1920:
   Canada's best kept military secret
   Halifax, Nova, Scotia
   Nimbus Publ. 1987

Sewell, Tony
    Garvey's children: The Legacy of Marcus Garvey
    Trenton, N.J. Africa World Press Inc.

Shreve, Dorothy Shadd
    The African Canadian Church: A Stabilizer
    Jordan Station, Ontario Paideia Press, 1983

Smucker, Barbara
    Underground to Canada.
    Toronto, Clarke, Irwin 1977

Thomson, Colin A.
    Blacks in Deep Snow: Black Pioneers in Canada.
    Don Mills, Dent & Sons 1979

Van Sertima, Ivan
    Great Black Leaders: ancient and modern New Brunswick
    N.J., Journal of African Civilizations Ltd. 1983

Walker, James W. St. G.,
    A History of Blacks in Canada:
    A Study guide for teachers and students
    Ottawa Minister of State Multiculturalism 1980

Young, Lisa
    Black Scientists
    New York, Facts on File, 1991

# BIBLIOGRAPHY AND OTHER SOURCES

Freedom Seekers by Daniel Hill

Contrast Publications

Share Publications

Ontario Black History Files

Spear Magazine

Black Theatre Canada- A Decade of Struggle by Lorraine Hubbard

First Baptist Church Anniversary Edition 1986

Apostle, Souvenir Edition-Jean Markham

Memory Book-Union United Church, Montreal

Fuse Magazine- A Historical Critique of Ontario Blacks by Leila Heath

The History of North Buxton Booklet by Arlie Robbins

Harry Jerome Awards Brochure- Black Business and Professional Association

National Congress of Black Women Brochure

Women of Our Times- Enid D'Oyley and Rella Braithwaite

The Black Business and Professional Women's Calendar by Tessa Benn Ireland

Southern Exposure Magazine, U.S.A.

An Historic minority  The Black people of Nova Scotia